Embodying Wesley's Catholic Spirit

Embodying Wesley's Catholic Spirit

Edited by
Daniel Castelo

☙PICKWICK *Publications* • Eugene, Oregon

EMBODYING WESLEY'S CATHOLIC SPIRIT

Copyright © 2017 Wipf and Stock Publishers. All rights reserved. Except for brief quotations in critical publications or reviews, no part of this book may be reproduced in any manner without prior written permission from the publisher. Write: Permissions, Wipf and Stock Publishers, 199 W. 8th Ave., Suite 3, Eugene, OR 97401.

Pickwick Publications
An Imprint of Wipf and Stock Publishers
199 W. 8th Ave., Suite 3
Eugene, OR 97401

www.wipfandstock.com

PAPERBACK ISBN: 978-1-62564-989-8
HARDCOVER ISBN: 978-1-4982-8524-7
EBOOK ISBN: 978-1-4982-4106-9

Cataloguing-in-Publication data:

Names: Castelo, Daniel, 1978–

Title: Embodying Wesley's Catholic spirit / edited by Daniel Castelo.

Description: Eugene, OR : Pickwick Publications, 2017 | Includes bibliographical references.

Identifiers: ISBN 978-1-62564-989-8 (paperback) | ISBN 978-1-4982-8524-7 (hardcover) | ISBN 978-1-4982-4106-9 (ebook)

Subjects: LCSH: Wesley, John, 1703–1791—Views on Catholic church. | Wesley, John, 1703–1791. | Catholic Church. | Methodist Church—Relations—Catholic Church—History—18th century.

Classification: BX8495.W5 E43 2017 (print) | BX8495.W5 E43 (ebook)

Manufactured in the U.S.A. MARCH 2, 2017

Contents

Introduction | vii

List of Contributors | xi

Abbreviations | xii

1 Negotiating Wesleyan Catholicity | 1
   Ted A. Campbell

2 American Methodism: A Contested Theological Tradition | 18
   Kevin M. Watson

3 The Non-Catholicity of a Catholic Spirit | 51
   D. Stephen Long

4 Wesley's Trinitarian Understanding of Holiness | 68
   Kenneth M. Loyer

5 Participating in Grace: Augustine and Wesley as Preachers of Sanctification | 87
   Scott Dermer

6 "The Complete Art of Happiness": Listening to the Sermon on the Mount with Wesley and Aquinas | 100
   Edgardo Colón-Emeric

7 John Calvin and John Wesley on Sanctification | 116
   Stephen W. Rankin

8 John Wesley and John Paul II on the Eucharist and Holiness | 133
   Stephen Sours

Bibliography | 153

Introduction

AT THE 45TH ANNUAL Meeting of the Wesleyan Theological Society held in March 2010 at Azusa Pacific University, a number of Wesleyan and Methodist scholars gathered together in response to a call I had sent in anticipation of the meeting. The original call was extended in the hopes of starting a conversation regarding the theological integrity of the Wesleyan-Methodist tradition. By "integrity" here I mean the degree to which Methodism can stand as a properly identifiable voice—as a theological tradition that can both contribute to and receive gifts from other theological traditions. Part of my concern stemmed from my seeing over the years Wesleyan and Methodist scholars being especially prone to assume various kinds of theological methodologies that would come and go within the academy. In particular, the movements of Boston personalism and process theology have had particularly strong Methodist representation and support over the years, developments which lead to the question: What is it about Methodism in particular that makes it prone to promote and adopt up-and-coming methodological innovations within the theological academy? Any number of hypotheses could be offered, but in terms of the call itself, I was interested not so much in answering this question as in showing Wesleyan-Methodist theology to be intricately embedded within what one could call a "catholic" tradition of Christian reflection.

At work in the original call was a sense of hope that the Wesleyan-Methodist movement is at a point now—especially given the significant work done over the past few decades—to stand on its own as a unique voice in theological conversations. The voice itself, as I saw it, stemmed from the tradition of the Wesleys but also moved beyond it. It involved a heritage that was at once ecclesial and revivalist. Seeing the number of projects being undertaken especially by younger scholars, I was encouraged that the

Introduction

time might be ripe for consolidating those sympathies somehow. And to my surprise, the feeling was shared: Close to twenty people responded to the original call in one way or another, and when we met at Azusa, we considered a number of ways to support one another and to make our general orientation known.

At this meeting, we decided to meet prior to future WTS meetings with the aim of putting a book together. Therefore, we met prior to the 46th (March 2011, Dallas), 47th (March 2012, Nashville), and 48th (March 2013, Seattle) Annual Meetings of WTS; furthermore, at the 48th, we had a dedicated panel at the meeting itself regarding the project. Most of the chapters in this volume found their first public expression in these settings. The theme eventually agreed upon for the book was the reclaiming and performance of a kind of "Wesleyan catholicity," and this with a focus on the theme of holiness, broadly understood. This topic was chosen given that this is one of the longstanding features of Wesleyan-Methodist theology. With this approach, we started to think about a book fleshed out in two major parts, which are represented here: 1) the consideration of catholicity in the Wesleyan-Methodist tradition, and 2) the engagement of other theological figures and movements from an explicit Wesleyan-Methodist location. The first part includes essays by Campbell, Watson, and Long; these represent different "takes" on the question of catholicity within the Methodist communion. Loyer's piece is a kind of dogmatic bridge into the second part, which has contributions by Dermer, Colón-Emeric, Rankin, and Sours.

Overall, the volume strives to show that the Wesleyan-Methodist tradition is one that can stand on its own in relation to other traditions and movements so as to receive and render charisms for the good of the Body of Christ. Yes, the way this tradition is interpreted and put to use can vary methodologically—such is the case with all traditions. At the same time, a reclaiming effort is always appropriate as well—a gesture *ad fontes* for the sake of present and future embodiments of the tradition. In this light, it is my hope that this book can be of aid to those who love, care, and wish to promote the Wesleyan-Methodist family of churches and its distinct witness.

I find it deeply satisfying to see this book come to print after such a long gestational period. I wish to thank all those interested in the project: those who came to the first and subsequent gatherings of the "Wesleyan Catholicity group," those who presented papers, and those who were

Introduction

willing to offer chapters to the volume in a subsequent phase. I have been deeply encouraged to work and engage colleagues who share the same passion that inspired the original call for the group. I would also like to extend my thanks to Wipf and Stock for being willing to assume this project into their Pickwick line. And finally, I wish to thank my home institution, Seattle Pacific University, because of its support in two ways: 1) a Faculty Research Grant offered by the Center for Scholarship and Faculty Development to cover some of the costs associated with the volume, as well as 2) the splendid aid of our theological librarian Steve Perisho, who helped me track down many items as part of the editing process.

Finally, I wish to dedicate this volume to Henry H. (Hal) Knight III, who was at the first meeting of this group and who has helped solidify the voice of Wesleyan-Methodist theology over many decades. Thank you, Hal, for your love and care toward the people called Methodists. Many of us—including myself, my wife and my father (all of us your students formally and informally)— have been deeply shaped by both your life and witness.

Daniel Castelo
Seattle, Washington

Contributors

Ted A. Campbell is Professor of Church History, Perkins School of Theology, Southern Methodist University.

Edgardo Colón-Emeric is Assistant Professor of Christian Theology, Duke University.

Scott Dermer is a PhD candidate, St. Louis University.

D. Stephen Long is Cary M. Maguire University Professor of Ethics, Southern Methodist University.

Kenneth M. Loyer is a United Methodist pastor and Adjunct Instructor of Theology at United Theological Seminary, Wesley Theological Seminary, and Messiah College.

Stephen Rankin is Chaplain and Minister to the University, Southern Methodist University.

Stephen Sours is Assistant Professor of Religion, Huntingdon College.

Kevin M. Watson is Assistant Professor of Wesleyan and Methodist Studies at the Candler School of Theology, Emory University.

Abbreviations

CSS: Wesley, John. "The Christian Sacrament and Sacrifice: Extracted from Dr. Brevint." In *Hymns on the Lord's Supper* by John and Charles Wesley, 3–32. Bristol, UK: Farley, 1745; facsimile ed.; Madison, NJ: Charles Wesley Society, 1995. Quotes have been slightly altered for stylistic purposes.

EE: John Paul II. *Ecclesia de Eucharistia*. http://w2.vatican.va/content/john-paul-ii/en/encyclicals/documents/hf_jp-ii_enc_20030417_eccl-de-euch.html.

HLS: Wesley, John and Charles. *Hymns on the Lord's Supper*. Madison: Charles Wesley Society, 1995.

In Johannis: Augustine. *In Johannis evangelium tractatus*. CCL 36. Turnhout: Brepols, 1954.

ST: Aquinas, Thomas. *The Summa Theologica of St. Thomas Aquinas*. Translated by the Fathers of the English Dominican Province. 5 vols. Allen, TX: Christian Classics, 1948.

Telford: Wesley, John. *The Letters of the Rev. John Wesley*. Edited by John Telford. 8 vols. London: Epworth, 1931.

WJW: Wesley, John. *The Bicentennial Edition of the Works of John Wesley*. Projected 35 vols. Nashville: Abingdon, 1976–.

Works: Wesley, John. *The Works of John Wesley*. 14 vols. 3rd, complete, and unabridged ed. 1872. Repr., Grand Rapids: Baker, 1979.

1

Negotiating Wesleyan Catholicity

Ted A. Campbell

*Meanwhile the church throughout Judea, Galilee,
and Samaria had peace and was built up*

(Acts 9:31, NRSV)

IT WAS A RARE moment in the Acts of the Apostles, as it has been through the long history of Christian communities, that the church "had peace and was built up." The author of this narrative of the expansion of Christian communities "in Jerusalem, in all Judea and Samaria, and to the ends of the earth" (Acts 1:8) paused in what we reckon as chapter 9 where the narrative recounted a fleeting moment of peace and edification as the Christian community reached the milestone, "throughout Judea, Galilee, and Samaria." Hidden from translations of this verse is the root of the words "catholic" and "catholicity": *kath' holēs*, translated "throughout" (NRSV) or "through all" (KJV/AV). The scope of the expression "catholic" would grow "to the ends of the earth" as it came to denote geographical extension of the Christian community through the fullness of the inhabited world.

"Catholic" would also come to denote the fullness (catholicity) of Christian teaching or doctrine shared throughout the world. The well-known quotation from St. Vincent of Lérins of the early fifth century encapsulates this understanding of "catholic": "[I]n the catholic church itself great care must be taken that we hold that which has been believed everywhere, always, by all. For this is truly and properly 'catholic.'"[1] St. Vincent's definition implied universality with respect to geography ("everywhere"), chronology ("always"), and perhaps greater diversities with the claim that the catholic faith has been believed "by all." His concern "that we hold that which has been *believed*" (my emphasis) in all of these ways shows that he considered catholicity as constituted, above all, by unity and universality in Christian teachings or doctrine.

The Church of England made a particular claim to catholicity in the age in which the Wesleyan movement emerged. Although the very idea of a national church contradicts the most basic, geographical meaning of catholicity, the Anglican way out of this contradiction has been to maintain that the Church of England is somehow "part of" the catholic church—the catholic church as it exists in England. This is expressed in the first sentence of the "Declaration of Assent" to which clergy of the Church of England subscribe: "The Church of England is part of the One, Holy, Catholic and Apostolic Church, worshipping the one true God, Father, Son and Holy Spirit."[2]

The understanding of the Church of England as a "part of" the *unam sanctam* had assumed a strongly territorial interpretation in the century or so before the origins of Methodism. This notion was grounded in canons of Christian ancient councils that forbade bishops, presbyters, and deacons from moving from one city (diocese) to another, exercising their ministerial authority within the region of another bishop, or "taking possession" of the diocese of another bishop.[3] Churches established by civil authority during the period of the reformations in the 1500s often took a similar view that the church established within the geographical bounds of a particular nation-state represented the universal church in that state. The territorial understanding of catholicity also became tied to national identities.

The situation was complicated in the British Isles. From the establishment of the united monarchy in 1707, the Church of England was established not for the United Kingdom as a whole but for England and Wales,

---

1. Vincent of Lérins, *Commonitorium*, 10; translation is my own.
2. In *Common Worship*, xi.
3. See "Council of Nicaea," canons 15–16 (13–14). The reference to "taking possession" of another bishop's diocese appears in a decree of the "Council of Ephesus," 68.

since the United Kingdom had also established the presbyterian Church of Scotland. Both of these ecclesial establishments reflected the principle of *cuius regio eius religio* that had prevailed in Europe since the age of the reformations, and the requirement that clergy swear their allegiance to the British Crown further underscored this understanding of the church. But the territorial and national understanding of catholicity implied in these civil establishments of religion was increasingly called into question by events in the 1680s and the 1780s.

The Act of Toleration of 1689 altered the territorial notion of Anglican catholicity by allowing alternate forms of Protestantism to function publicly within restrictions specified in the Act. Within the bounds of these restrictions–for example, registration of Dissenting chapels, subscription to the "doctrinal part" of the Thirty-Nine Articles, keeping doors and windows of chapels open during assemblies–Quakers, Baptists, Congregationalists, and Presbyterians (shorn of presbyteries by another provision of the Act) could conduct public worship within the geographical bounds of Anglican dioceses and parishes in England and Wales. The ideology of toleration enunciated by John Locke that immediately followed the Toleration Act served further to question the epistemological basis for a single ecclesial establishment. By the time John and Charles Wesley began their ministries, England and Wales no longer had the outward appearance of one catholic church.

An even more critical challenge to the territorial and national notion of catholicity followed the British recognition of US independence in 1783, when Church of England clergy could no longer function in parishes in the United States given their sworn allegiance to a foreign political state. A territory with congregations founded by the Church of England now existed in which the territorial claim to catholicity made by the Church of England could not function. A precedent that helped North American Anglicans in this situation was the Scottish Episcopalians Act of 1711 that had allowed for the separate existence of an Episcopal Church alongside the established Church of Scotland. This complicated the claim to territorial catholicity even further, allowing a non-established version of the same ecclesial body in the United Kingdom that was simultaneously established as the national Church of England. The fact that the Scottish Episcopal Church did not require an oath of allegiance to the reigning monarch on the part of its clergy allowed that church to consecrate Samuel Seabury as the first bishop of the Protestant Episcopal Church in the USA.

The same crisis of territorial catholicity in the 1780s forced Wesleyan communities to deal with issues of their identification as distinct ecclesial communities apart from the Church of England and to negotiate their own identities as catholic Christian communities. In Britain as well as the United States this led to an uneven cluster of ecclesial claims among Wesleyan groups. Recurrent schisms and unions through the histories of Methodist communities have forced renewed negotiations of the meaning of catholicity, and the likelihood of new divisions in our times calls once again for reconsideration of the senses in which Wesleyan communities can claim catholicity.

This chapter will examine the inheritance of Anglican catholicity in the early Wesleyan movement, John Wesley's challenges to the inherited notion of territorial catholicity, the claims to catholicity that the earliest Wesleyan church (the Methodist Episcopal Church) made, and some prospects for a renewed and ecumenically responsible sense of Wesleyan catholicity today.

Catholicity and the Origins of the Wesleyan Movement

The focus of the nascent Wesleyan movement in the decades prior to the 1780s was not on issues of sacramental authority, ordinations, and the definition of broader church doctrine that might challenge inherited understandings of catholicity. In these earlier decades, the movement focused overwhelmingly on the cultivation of Christian holiness, implying a limited number of doctrinal claims that John Wesley took to be consistent with historic catholic definitions of Christian teachings, and a related series of practices that did not even appear to challenge the catholicity claimed by the Church of England with the critical exception of itinerant preaching. That is to say, the Wesleyan movement up to the mid-1780s functioned largely within an inherited Anglican understanding of catholicity. This can be seen by considering the characteristic doctrines and practices advocated by the Wesleyan movement in this early period.

John Wesley's sermon on a "Catholic Spirit" (1749) enunciated his view that unity in the faith depended on a relatively small core of essential or fundamental doctrines, though the sermon itself did not specify these.[4] Wesley's "Letter to a Roman Catholic," written within months of "Catholic Spirit," did specify a number of doctrines shared between Protestant

---

4. Wesley, "Catholic Spirit," 92–94.

churches and the Catholic Church.⁵ Based on this letter, his later edition of the Articles of Religion, and statements scattered throughout his writings, we might venture that he considered the following essential or fundamental doctrines to have universal or catholic status within Christian communities:

- The worship of, and doctrine about, the holy Trinity;
- The doctrine of the full divinity of Jesus Christ;
- The doctrine of the atonement and its concomitant belief in the full humanity of Jesus Christ;
- The doctrine of the final authority of the scriptures in matters related to salvation and to the reform of the church;
- The doctrine of original sin and its implication of the universal need for divine grace, though noting Wesley's reservations about the teaching that original sin itself warranted damnation on the part of all human beings (see below on this matter);
- The doctrine of justification by faith alone, though noting Wesley's sense in which good works might be considered "remotely" necessary to final salvation;
- The doctrine of regeneration and sanctification following from it;
- The doctrine of the church.

In addition to these common teachings, John Wesley seemed to have thought that the practices of baptism and the Lord's Supper were essential Christian practices, thus adding to the previous list:

- The practice and the doctrine of baptism;
- The practice and doctrine of the Lord's Supper.⁶

John Wesley's understanding of the term "catholic" expressed in the sermon "Catholic Spirit" and implied in this restricted list of essentials involved a degree of liberality that allowed for differences of "opinions" and "modes of worship" that could be tolerated within and between Christian communities.

It is revealing to contrast these generally affirmed "catholic" teachings and practices with the distinctive doctrines championed by the early

---

5. See Wesley, "Letter to a Roman Catholic, 18 July 1749."

6. On these points, see Campbell, *Wesleyan Beliefs*, chap. 1; as well as Williams, *John Wesley's Theology Today*, 16–17.

Methodist movement. John Wesley wrote in 1746, "Our main doctrines, which include all the rest, are three, that of repentance, of faith, and of holiness."[7] Here there are no doctrinal definitions about God, Jesus Christ, the divine Trinity, or the Christian church and its sacraments. The quotation given here appears in a tract entitled "The Principles of a Methodist Farther Explained," and the expression "our main doctrines" in this sentence indicates its scope: it is not a claim about what is necessary for the unity of a Christian church in the broader or catholic sense; rather, it is a claim about the distinct mission or apostolate of the Methodist movement under Wesley's leadership. The scope of these doctrinal claims is not "catholic"; it is restricted to the mission of this particular movement in its particular time and place.

This quotation echoes a series of claims made by John Wesley about the distinctive teachings of the Methodist movement and even the broader Evangelical movement of his day. Wesley consistently pointed to a threefold cluster of doctrines roughly as follows:

- The doctrine of original sin and its implication of repentance, implying the acknowledgment of one's need for divine help or grace;
- The doctrine of justification by faith in Christ, with the concomitant notion that true faith implied affective engagement with as well as intellectual assent to the Gospel message and often with an accompanying claim of the normative nature of an experience of the assurance of pardon; and
- The doctrine of sanctification (growth in holiness) following justification, with the specific claim in the Wesleyan movement of the possibility of entire sanctification prior to death.[8]

If this cluster of teachings was distinctive of the Wesleyan movement and the broader Evangelical movement in Wesley's time, Wesley himself

---

7. "The Principles of a Methodist Farther Explained," 227.

8. The following three references in addition to the quotation above from "The Principles of a Methodist Farther Explained" also identify this cluster of three doctrines: 1) "Letter to George Downing, 6 April 1761" where Wesley refers to "the three grand scriptural doctrines, original sin, justification by faith, and holiness consequent thereon" (250); 2) Wesley's sermon on "The Means of Grace" where he claimed that the means of grace are "the ordinary channels whereby [God] might convey to men, preventing, justifying, or sanctifying grace" (378 and 381); and 3) Wesley's sermon on "The Scripture Way of Salvation," 156–60. On this cluster of doctrines, see Campbell, *Wesleyan Beliefs*, 73–77.

maintained that the doctrines were in no way novel; they reflected the teachings of "the whole church in the purest ages."[9] In other words, he understood this cluster of doctrines to be a subset of catholic doctrine, a subset that needed to be emphasized and renewed in his time because of the long neglect of these teachings.

Similarly, the early Wesleyan movement involved an interlocking series of distinctive practices, all but one of which could be seen as subsisting within the catholicity claimed by the Church of England. The one exception not consistent with the Church of England's sense of catholicity was itinerant preaching (see immediately below), but the Wesleyan classes, bands, societies, and other structures (for example, benevolent institutions) did not pose a threat to the catholicity of the Church of England. In fact, the Methodist "United Societies" regularized in the General Rules (from 1743) specifically interlocked with the parish structures of the Church of England in the requirement that members of the Wesleyan societies should attend "the public worship of God," including both parts of the Sunday observance ideally if not typically practiced in Anglican congregations, namely "the ministry of the Word, either read or expounded" (in the Morning Prayer and Evening Prayer services) and "The Supper of the Lord."[10] The Wesleyan bands, classes, and larger societies did not require clergy for their regular work. They were led locally by class and band leaders and by the stewards of the local societies.

John Wesley's Challenges to Territorial Catholicity

Itinerant preaching was the one practice of the early Wesleyan movement that conflicted with the territorial prerogatives claimed by the Church of England. When challenged on the matter of extra-parochial preaching by Bishop Joseph Butler of Bristol, John Wesley expressed a typically Anglican understanding of the universality or catholicity of the church when he stated, "Your lordship knows, being ordained a priest, by the commission then received I am a priest of the Church Universal."[11] But Wesley took this to mean that he could preach within the bounds of a diocese to which he was not responsible and within the bounds of a parish in which another

---

9. Wesley, "On Laying the Foundation of the New Chapel, Near the City-Road, London," 586.

10. Wesley, "The Nature, Design, and General Rules of the United Societies," 73.

11. "Wesley's Interview with Bishop Butler," 472.

priest had been installed as spiritual leader. This violated the territorial understanding of catholicity embraced by the Church of England but it is quite consistent with the claim involved in Wesley's well-known assertion,

> I look upon *all the world* as *my parish*; thus far I mean, that in whatever part of it I am, I judge it meet, right, and my bounden duty, to declare unto all that are willing to hear the glad tidings of salvation.[12]

This is consistent with Wesley's vision of spreading the Gospel in expanding contiguous regions, sometimes citing Acts 1:8 ("in Jerusalem, in all Judea and Samaria, and to the ends of the earth") as his explicit scriptural grounds for this vision.[13]

But if a vision of geographical expansion served as Wesley's grounds for the practice of itinerant preaching, this vision increasingly collided with the territorial vision of catholicity practiced within existing diocesan and parochial structures of the Church of England and formally embedded in Anglican doctrine. The Methodist use of lay preachers conflicted explicitly with the Twenty-third Article of Religion of the Church of England, which stated,

> It is not lawful for any man to take upon him the office of public preaching or ministering the sacraments in the congregation, before he be lawfully called and sent to execute the same. And those we ought to judge lawfully called and sent, which be chosen and called to this work by men who have public authority given unto them in the congregation to call and send ministers into the Lord's vineyard.[14]

The Act of Toleration of 1689 had extended the limits of this provision to allow preaching in registered Dissenting churches, but the Toleration Act did not explicitly allow for the itineration of a priest of the Church of England within a parish in which he was not installed, nor did it sanction the work of lay preachers who were communicants of the Church of England.

It was on this matter of itinerant preaching that John and Charles Wesley fundamentally differed beginning in the 1750s. Charles's branch of the Wesleyan movement, which Gareth Lloyd identifies as "Church Methodists," rejected itinerant preaching, insisting on compliance with the Articles

---

12. Journal Entry "11 June 1739," 67.
13. See Campbell, "John Wesley on the Mission of the Church," 56–57.
14. "*The Thirty-Nine Articles* of the Church of England," Article 23 (534).

and canons of the Church of England as well as such national legislation as the Toleration Act that governed church activities.[15] Though consistently claiming his fidelity to the national church, John pursued an increasingly independent trajectory in which missional priorities would trump ecclesial norms and territorial claims in the matter of itinerant preaching and eventually in such other matters as the Church of England canons concerning ordinations. John was beginning to throw off the notion of territorial catholicity in place of which he offered a different understanding of church implying a significantly different understanding of the church's catholicity.

Another instance illustrates John Wesley's willingness to operate within the territorial prerogatives of Anglican bishops and clergy, and this is in his relationship with the Greek Bishop Gerasimos Avlonites (Erasmus Aulonita) in the early 1760s. John Wesley recognized Gerasimos's identity as a bishop and Gerasimos's authority to ordain Wesley's London assistant John Jones in the spring of 1764.[16] But this ordination was undertaken within the diocese of the Bishop of London, thus violating the canons of the First Council of Nicaea (supposing Gerasimos to have recognized the Bishop of London as the legitimate bishop in this area) and violating the prerogative of an Anglican bishop within his own diocese.

One of the Wesleys' London leaders, John Richardson, expressed to Charles Wesley his reservations about Jones's ordination in a way that presupposed the territorial and national prerogatives of the Church of England:

> a Greek bishop (or one supposed to be so), comes into England and exercises the office of ordination, not among his own countrymen, or those of his own church, but among English people and them of the Established Church who have no connexion with, or dependence upon the Greek church.[17]

Richardson's letter indicated that he would not recognize Gerasimos's authority as a bishop when acting in England and among English people even if Richardson had conceded the authenticity of Gerasimos's claim to be Bishop of Arkadia. In this complicated case, John Wesley would later repudiate ordinations that Gerasimos performed for Evangelical clergy who did not understand Greek and for which Gerasimos expected a fee for his expenses. But in the case of John Jones, who did understand the

---

15. See Lloyd, *Charles Wesley and the Struggle for Methodist Identity*, 147–61, 180–212, and 219–33.

16. See Campbell, "The Transgressions of Gerasimos Avlonites."

17. Richardson, "Letter to Charles Wesley, 13 March 1764."

Embodying Wesley's Catholic Spirit

Greek language in which the ordination was carried out, and for whose ordination Gerasimos apparently required no fee (perhaps as a courtesy to Wesley?), Wesley recognized the Greek bishop's ordination even though it occurred within the diocese of the Bishop of London. Similarly, John Wesley expected others to recognize his own ministries across diocesan and parochial boundaries consistent with his earlier claim to "look upon all the world as [his] parish."

Wesley's ordinations of 1784 provide a case in which he explicitly appealed to a notion of shifting territorial and national boundaries as a ground for his actions. Wesley stated that his reading of Peter King convinced him that presbyters have "an inherent right to ordain" since presbyters (elders, priests) and bishops were of the same ministerial *order*, and although bishops had been consecrated to a higher degree than their fellow presbyters and should normally ordain, presbyters could ordain in exceptional cases such as the case Wesley perceived in North America.[18] For a long stretch in the Middle Ages, in fact, the Catholic Church had spoken of the *ordination* of sub-deacons, deacons, and priests, and the *consecration* of bishops, and the Church of England had continued this naming convention, though there was neither Catholic nor Anglican precedent for ordination being performed by a priest.[19]

Wesley addressed the issues of territoriality and nationality in the *apologia* he wrote to justify his ordinations:

> But the case is widely different between England and North America. Here there are bishops who have a legal jurisdiction. In America there are none, neither any parish ministers, so that for some hundred miles together there is none either to baptize or to administer the Lord's Supper. Here, therefore, my scruples are at an end, and I conceive myself at full liberty, as I violate no order and invade no man's right by appointing and sending labourers into the harvest.[20]

The territorial notion of catholicity was at stake at this moment in the transition from a Methodist movement to a Methodist church. Wesley's letter made some stringent points. In the past, the provincial churches had been under the authority of the Bishop of London, but Wesley considered the British acknowledgment of US independence to imply that the Church

---

18. "To 'Our Brethren in America,'" 83.
19. See Stuhlman, *Occasions of Grace*, 263.
20. "To 'Our Brethren in America,'" 83.

of England no longer had any jurisdiction in the former provinces. His actions therefore "violate[d] no order, and invade[d] no man's right," that is, they did not usurp the authority of the Bishop of London since the Church of England no longer held legal authority in the US. In fact, he went on to say that he had asked the Bishop of London to ordain one of his preachers for the North American work, and the bishop refused. This strengthened his claim that his own actions did not usurp the authority of the Bishop of London. Though this is not stated in the letter, Wesley's actions in this case were strictly for America, and the ministers ordained and consecrated did not exercise their ministries until they came to America. Wesley's actions violated the canons of the Church of England regarding ordinations; he admitted as much in the letter: "I was [in the past] determined *as little as possible* to violate the established order of the national Church to which I belonged" (my emphasis). But he was convinced that the situation in the United States made the territorial claims of the Church of England invalid in the new situation.

This would have a very significant effect on American Methodist conceptions of the catholic nature of the church. Consistent with the non-establishment clause that would be enshrined in the US Bill of Rights when ratified in 1789, American Methodism would have to construe its identity as a part of the one catholic church in a very different way than the territorial interpretation favored in Europe and in the Church of England in particular. John Wesley's early rejection of those territorial claims blazed a path that would lead to this challenge to territorial catholicity.

Claims to Catholicity on the Part of the Methodist Episcopal Church

How, then, did the newly established Methodist Episcopal Church claim its catholic identity? The Christmas Conference of 1784, presided over by Thomas Coke, whom John Wesley had consecrated as superintendent, made a series of decisions within a few days' time that implied and in some cases explicitly stated catholic claims on the part of the new ecclesial community. The Conference approved 1) *The Sunday Service of the Methodists in North America* as its authorized liturgy, 2) Twenty-Five Articles of Religion as its authorized doctrine, and 3) a series of Minutes laying out the shape of its ecclesial polity. Although John Wesley had edited the *Sunday Service* from the Book of Common Prayer, had edited twenty-four of the Twenty-Five

Articles from the Thirty-Nine Articles of the Church of England, and had generally enunciated the material in the earlier Minutes that would be distilled by Coke and Asbury and approved at the Christmas Conference, we have to credit the Christmas Conference itself as authorizing these three foundational documents.

Let us observe, then, some of the key elements of this relatively simple, new church order. In the first place, neither the *Sunday Service* nor the Twenty-Five Articles had any reference to distinctive Methodist teachings or practices: no watch nights, no love feasts, and no references to teachings about universal prevenient grace, the assurance of pardon, or entire sanctification. They offered a simple, catholic vision of church within which distinctive Wesleyan teachings and practices could continue.

The liturgical vision of the *Sunday Service* and in Wesley's accompanying letter reflected in many respects the existing parochial patterns of the Church of England, involving the use of the liturgies for Morning Prayer, the Lord's Supper, and Evening Prayer every Sunday, and the Great Litany on Wednesdays and Fridays, though it called for *extempore* prayer on Mondays, Tuesdays, Thursdays, and Saturdays.[21] The *Sunday Service* removed Prayer Book references to saints' days but retained the christological cycle of the liturgical year with a three-page lectionary giving readings for each Sunday organized into the seasons of Advent, Christmas, Easter, Whitsunday (Pentecost), Trinity Sunday, and "Sundays after Trinity Sunday" (ordinary time), with collects and epistle and Gospel lessons for each Sunday printed in full.[22] The Twenty-Five Articles adopted by the Christmas Conference included a lukewarm affirmation of infant baptism ("The baptism of young children is to be retained in the Church") though the *Sunday Service*, following the pattern of the Prayer Book, privileged infant baptism as a normative practice by placing the ritual for infant baptism first before the baptism of persons of "riper years."[23]

The ordinal provided in the *Sunday Service* continued the Anglican language of "making" deacons, "ordaining" elders (BCP "priests"), and "consecrating" superintendents (BCP "bishops").[24] Despite this, a rubric

---

21. Ibid., 83–84.

22. *John Wesley's Sunday Service*, 3–5 (unnumbered) and 27–124; Epiphany and Lent are not identified as separate seasons in the lectionary.

23. Ibid.: the service for "The Ministration of Baptism of Infants" is given on 139–43 and the service for "The Ministration of Baptism to Such as Are of Riper Years" is given on 143–49.

24. Ibid., 280–305, headings on 280, 285, and 296.

accompanying the liturgy for the consecration of superintendents in the *Sunday Service* spoke of the laying-on of hands of "the Superintendent [singular] and Elders present," probably envisioning the singular moment when Thomas Coke and elders present would consecrate Francis Asbury as a superintendent. But in this respect the liturgy of the newly founded church did not continue the patristic, Orthodox, Catholic, and Anglican requirement that at least three bishops needed to be present for the consecration of another bishop.[25]

The Christmas Conference added to the Articles edited by Wesley an article affirming their allegiance to the government of the United States, a concession to territorial and national identity that has proven highly problematic as successor churches have become global entities.[26]

Many of the items that Wesley and the Christmas Conference omitted from the Prayer Book reflected specific concerns of the Evangelical movement. For example, the *Sunday Service* omitted the most explicit reference to the regeneration of infants in baptism, the prayer of thanksgiving that began, "Seeing now, dearly beloved brethren, that this child is regenerate and grafted into the body of Christs [sic] Church . . ."[27] Perhaps consistent with this omission, the version of the Articles of Religion endorsed by the Christmas Conference retained the claim that baptism is "a sign of regeneration, or the new birth," but omitted material in the Article on baptism utilizing strongly instrumental language:

> whereby, as by an instrument, they that receive baptism rightly are grafted into the church, the promises of forgiveness of sin, and our adoption to be the sons of God, by the Holy Ghost, are visibly signed and sealed[28]

Where the Prayer Book specified that infants should be "dipped," that is, immersed, unless they were gravely ill, the *Sunday Service* provided for immersion or sprinkling.[29] The earliest editions of the *Sunday Service* included

---

25. Ibid., 303.

26. See "*The Articles of Religion* of the Methodist Episcopal Church," Article 23 (207).

27. Cummings, *The Book of Common Prayer*, 412; compare to *John Wesley's Sunday Service*, 142, which has, "Seeing now, dearly beloved brethren, that this Child is grafted into the body of Christ's Church . . .," omitting "regenerate and."

28. "*The Thirty-Nine Articles* of the Church of England," Article 27 (535); "*The Articles of Religion* of the Methodist Episcopal Church," Article 17 (205).

29. Cummings, *The Book of Common Prayer*, 412; compare to *John Wesley's Sunday Service*, 142 and 148 (for adults).

the sign of the cross in the service of baptism, though later versions omitted it.[30] The *Sunday Service* omitted the catechism and the rite of confirmation altogether. This has puzzled some Methodist interpreters, though I suspect that Wesley thought of the catechetical process as being better served by his own *Instructions for Children* and the processes of the Methodist General Rules, societies, and bands than the traditional processes of Christian initiation envisioned in the Prayer Book Catechism and its service for confirmation. The service for the Lord's Supper omitted the Nicene Creed, and the Christmas Conference adopted Wesley's revision of the Articles of Religion omitting the Article that affirmed the "Three Creeds" (Apostles' Creed, Nicene Creed, and Athanasian Creed), leaving American Methodists with the Apostles' Creed only, in the service of Morning Prayer.[31] These particular omissions were not "catholic" in the sense of a high-church orientation, but they were arguably "catholic" insofar as they allowed wider latitude in beliefs and practices. That is to say, they were "catholic" in John Wesley's sense of a "Catholic Spirit."

Two items that Wesley and the Christmas Conference omitted from the Articles of Religion allowed a vision of catholicity that was in specific respects less Western and Augustinian than their Anglican precedents. The Anglican Article on original sin expressed the Augustinian belief that original sin itself warranted damnation for all humans subsequent to Adam and Eve, but Wesley omitted the phrase, "and therefore in every person born into this world, it [original sin] deserveth God's wrath and damnation."[32] Given Wesley's privately expressed reservations about whether any humans would be damned on the basis of original sin alone,[33] this omission should not be seen as merely reducing the verbiage of the Articles. An omission did not amount to a denial, but it left the matter doctrinally undefined and thus open to a latitude of interpretations. Wesley and the Christmas Conference also omitted the entire Anglican Article on predestination,[34]

30. Cummings, *The Book of Common Prayer*, 412; compare to *John Wesley's Sunday Service*, 142; but notice *The Sunday Service of the Methodists with Other Occasional Services*, 145, where the rubric for signing and the prayer accompanying the signing are omitted.

31. The Apostles' Creed is given in the service for Morning Prayer in *John Wesley's Sunday Service*, 12.

32. "*The Thirty-Nine Articles* of the Church of England," Article 9 (531); "*The Articles of Religion* of the Methodist Episcopal Church," Article 7 (203).

33. See "Letter to John Mason, 21 November 1776."

34. "*The Thirty-Nine Articles* of the Church of England," Article 17 (532–33); "*The Articles of Religion* of the Methodist Episcopal Church," where it is absent.

again omitting the most distinctively Western interpretation of the work of divine grace and opening a larger range of interpretations.

In fact, the omissions in the Articles of Religion and the *Sunday Service* were neither to deny the doctrinal teachings omitted nor to rule out the practices omitted. That is to say, the omission of the Article on predestination did not constitute a denial of the doctrine of predestination; it simply left the matter open to local and individual interpretations. Similarly, the omission of the signing in baptism did not prohibit the practice but meant that it was no longer an authorized or mandated practice, and thus was open to decisions of local communities or (more likely) of individual clergy performing baptisms. In the particular sense of catholicity enunciated in Wesley's sermon on "Catholic Spirit," these omissions opened up the range of catholicity by allowing broader interpretations of teachings and practices.

Prospects for Wesleyan Catholicity Today

The vision of catholic faith that had been inherited from the Church of England, that evolved in early Methodist societies, and that was negotiated in the nascent Methodist Episcopal Church was a daringly simple vision consistent with Wesley's admonition to the American Methodists that they should be "at full liberty, simply to follow the Scriptures and the primitive church."[35] It allowed Wesleyan communities to function as a church with a recognizably catholic vision, yet continuing within that church the distinctive doctrinal emphases and distinctive practices of the Wesleyan movement.

More than two hundred years have passed since these understandings of catholicity were negotiated in early Wesleyan communities. The liturgical vision of the *Sunday Service* has given way in many nominally Wesleyan communities to services that reflect more the performance culture of Victorian-era music halls with Gospel music and a long harangue by an orator, or that reflect contemporary rock and roll performance culture with Contemporary Christian music and a brief talk by a pastor on a four-legged stool. Either scenario lacks the elements of historic catholic liturgical and sacramental practice inherited from the Book of Common Prayer and envisioned in the *Sunday Service*. Wesley's admonition that elders should administer the sacrament of the Lord's Supper every Lord's Day may have been followed literally by early itinerant clergy in the Methodist Episcopal

---

35. "To 'Our Brethren in America,'" 83–84.

Church, but local societies did not see clergy weekly and grew accustomed to far less frequent administration of the sacrament. Distinctively Wesleyan doctrinal emphases such as the goal of entire sanctification, practices such as the use of the General Rules enforced in bands and classes, and the practice of truly itinerant (parish-boundary-ignoring) ministry began to disappear from Wesleyan churches from the late 1800s.

In short, it has been increasingly difficult to sustain a Wesleyan vision of Christian catholicity within the context of existing Wesleyan churches. We seem always to be battling uphill against external and popular winds of doctrine and worship practices. I suppose that the communities with Wesleyan roots who have taken the path described in the previous paragraph might argue that they are extending Wesley's own extensions of the limits of catholicity, but those of us who passionately desire a more specifically Wesleyan vision of catholicity informed by the wisdom of ancient and ecumenical Christian insights find ourselves increasingly frustrated with ever-more-diffuse doctrinal and liturgical commitments (or lack thereof) of our denominations.

Perhaps we have erred in thinking that Wesleyan renewal—especially a renewal of a Wesleyan catholic vision—will occur in historically Wesleyan denominations that now seemed to be hardened against the renewal of such a vision. We seem to have at least three broad options available:

a. Struggle to embody a Wesleyan catholic vision within existing Wesleyan denominations;

b. Move to more historically catholic denominations (Anglican, Catholic, Orthodox) and try to embody Wesleyan distinctives in doctrine and practices within them; or

c. Form a new denominational body or bodies.

Each of these options has its particular perils. The last thing we should envision if we want to embody a catholic Christian vision is yet another denomination or another series of denominations (option c). The frustrations of cohabiting denominational space with colleagues whose vision of Christian faith is not catholic in any of the senses described here (option a) has been described above. Other denominations with a catholic vision (option b) might allow a distinctive emphasis on the cultivation of holiness in small groups with something like the General Rules, but almost certainly could not allow anything like the Wesleyan vision of itineration across the parishes of existing congregations of those denominations. That is to say, they might allow for a "charleswesleyan" but not a "johnwesleyan" understanding of distinctive Wesleyanism.

A fourth option (option d) would be to form *an interim ecclesial community existing across the boundaries of current denominational structures*, focused on a Wesleyan vision of catholic Christian faith as it searches for a more permanent denominational home or homes. This option would have its own perils. All of the critical issues facing our denominations today would follow us into such an interim structure. Should a specific teaching on homosexuality be enshrined as a necessary element of a catholic Christian vision? I would say no, but I suspect that others would disagree strongly. Should we continue the full inclusion of women in ordained ministry in such a vision of catholic faith? I would insist on it, but again I suspect that others (who would opt for a properly Catholic or Orthodox vision of catholicity) would say no. Should constituents of this new interim ecclesial community proceed to organize new congregations or ordain clergy apart from existing denominational structures? I would be of a divided mind on those issues, but I suspect that they and a host of others would prove to be divisive. An interim community might not have to solve all those issues immediately. Yet another peril is that "option d" is very often the way to "option c": groups seldom begin by deliberately starting new denominations; they form alliances or fellowships and some years later they realize that they are *de facto* separate.

It is a tempting option, though, if for no other reason than to claim for ourselves a current of contemporary Wesleyan life seeking a more catholic vision of Christian faith and practice. I have found the vigorous conversations on the "Sacramental Nazarenes" (formerly "Liturgical Nazarenes") Facebook page to be enormously encouraging as a sign of broad interest in such a Wesleyan catholic vision. Those discussions also make me aware of the issues likely to divide those of us who might pursue a more formal structure envisioned above for pursuing such a vision.

"Meanwhile the church throughout Judea, Galilee, and Samaria had peace and was built up" (Acts 9:31). May almighty God make it so in our time, even if for a lovely, fleeting moment.

2

American Methodism
A Contested Theological Tradition

Kevin M. Watson

Is AMERICAN METHODISM a coherent theological tradition? Over the past half-century, interpreters of the Wesleyan tradition have struggled with the task of defining and delineating it. In the 1960s, Robert E. Chiles began his landmark study of shifts in American Methodist theology by asking, "Is the history of Methodist theology the story of a fall from the perfection of a Wesleyan Eden into a world of theological defection?"[1] Chiles argued that "the loss of theological truth through willful distortion or deliberate desertion is comparatively rare; it does not reflect intellectual obtuseness or spiritual perversity as much as it does the committed effort of the theologian to speak a language meaningful for his day."[2] On Chiles's account, there is "a certain inevitability about the compromises in a theological tradition."[3]

In the 1980s, Thomas Langford shifted from discussing the Methodist tradition to focusing on the Wesleyan tradition.[4] Langford argued that

1. Chiles, *Theological Transition in American Methodism*, 13.
2. Ibid.
3. Ibid., 15.
4. "Wesleyan" and "Methodist" are often used interchangeably, which creates some difficulty in identifying who is included in the tradition. In this essay, I use the terms the authors themselves use in interacting with their work. In general, I prefer "Methodist,"

there was indeed continuity and consistency within developments in the Wesleyan tradition. Langford defined a "historical stream" as a tradition if "it possesses dominant characteristics and conveys an enduring sense of meaning."[5] The Wesleyan tradition met Langford's criteria because "its point of origin is clear and its dominant current can be traced rather well."[6] However, Langford also conceded that "the stream does not have neat boundaries."[7]

Most recently, Jason E. Vickers has added further to the case for Methodism persisting as a coherent theological tradition. Vickers's account is not only descriptive but shifts to being prescriptive, arguing for the need for the dogmatic development of Methodism as a theological tradition. Similar to Langford, Vickers emphasizes continuity and consistency in American Methodism, seeing it as "a living and dynamic theological tradition in which five distinct languages are spoken."[8] Vickers identifies these five languages as "evangelicalism, radicalism, ecumenism, liberalism, and Wesleyanism," and further argues that all five "have been present from the beginning, though in varying degrees."[9] Vickers then surveys several contemporary American Methodist theologians, such as Catherine Keller and William Abraham, arguing that most "are truly multi-lingual in their approach, combining three or more of these languages."[10] For Vickers it is "the sheer variety of combinations that have emerged in recent years [that] reflects the extent to which American Methodist theology is truly a dynamic and living tradition."[11]

---

as it designates the movement and the churches that arose from it, instead of the key founder of the movement. But I also see the two terms as generally synonymous.

5. Langford, *Practical Divinity*, 11.

6. Ibid., 12.

7. Ibid.

8. Vickers, "American Methodism," 33. A notable exception to the general agreement among recent historical theologians of Methodism as a theological tradition is William J. Abraham. In 2005, Abraham argued that Wesley "created and let loose a tradition that from the beginning was unstable. Like it or not, he inspired a network of ecclesial communities that fostered a latitudinarianism that he himself vehemently rejected . . . The plethora of historical Wesleys signals the end of Wesleyan theology" ("The End of Wesleyan Theology," 15).

9. Vickers, "American Methodism," 33.

10. Ibid., 34.

11. Ibid.

Embodying Wesley's Catholic Spirit

The general agreement that there is a recognizable and coherent American Methodist theological tradition is somewhat surprising given the frequent divisions throughout the history of Methodism in America, as well as the significant divisions that currently exist across the Wesleyan/Methodist family. When the various splits, separations, reunions, and mergers are all counted, there are at least thirty distinct denominations that have existed throughout the history of American Methodism.[12] And yet, the previous accounts are all quite optimistic about the possibilities for the ongoing vitality of American Methodist theology. Vickers, in particular, not only describes the existence of a variety of "languages" in American Methodist theology but also prescribes a multi-lingual approach as an essential norm going forward in order to develop American Methodism as a dogmatic tradition.

The attempt to describe a theological tradition over more than two centuries is inevitably difficult. In doing so, the historian is faced with the difficult question of whether tensions within the tradition strain the ability to meaningfully identify a coherent tradition. Vickers, for example, makes a strong case for the way in which Methodism has persisted as a kind of family feud, where the argument itself in some sense constitutes the tradition.[13] And still, there are challenges with such an approach. For example, the languages Vickers identifies are not stable throughout the history of American Methodism. This instability introduces more ambiguity than clarity in the attempt to identify a coherent theological tradition. "Radical," for example, means something quite different for Wesley than it does for B. T. Roberts. And neither Wesley nor Roberts would recognize the way the term is used today by contemporary theologians who are Methodist. Another challenge is that a multi-lingual approach to Methodist theology mutes the voices of historical figures who passionately disagreed with each other about what it meant to be Methodist or Wesleyan (and whether these words meant the same thing). Some of these would not necessarily have

---

12. This is illustrated nicely in the chart on display in Richey, Rowe, and Schmidt, *The Methodist Experience in America*, 2:21.

13. The comfort with deep tension existing within a theological tradition resonates with the work of Alasdair MacIntyre, who sees a tradition itself as "an argument extended through time in which certain fundamental agreements are defined and redefined" (MacIntyre, *Whose Justice? Which Rationality?*, 12). In a phone conversation I had with him, Vickers specifically connected MacIntyre's understanding of a tradition to his work in "American Methodism."

seen being multi-lingual as a virtue.[14] How would a multi-lingual approach account for B. T. Roberts's expulsion from the Methodist Episcopal Church in 1858 for "immoral and unchristian conduct" due to his accusation that the Genesee Conference of the MEC was promoting a new kind of Methodism that was not actually sufficiently Methodist?[15] On my reading of Vickers's work, the imagery he uses seems to imply that the various languages could simply be translated so that they mean essentially the same thing. This may be a use of the image that Vickers did not intend, but it suggests the potential to overlook the specific arguments Methodists throughout history have had with one another. These historical figures thought they understood one another perfectly well and nevertheless deeply disagreed with one another. Finally, Vickers's agenda for the dogmatic development of Methodism seems to lead to a prioritization of a theoretical construct for Methodist dogmatics over historical precision.[16] Vickers's account of Methodism as a theological tradition awaiting dogmatic development through an approach that speaks "evangelical," "radical," "ecumenical," "liberal," and "Wesleyan" languages advances Albert C. Outler's big tent theological vision for the newly constituted United Methodist Church more effectively than it provides a survey of the actual history of developments, changes, and even fragmentations in the history of American Methodist theology. For instance, it provides a way to secure unity in one church for both those who see themselves as theologically liberal and evangelical. The disadvantage is that it requires people to hold their convictions loosely, perhaps in a way that does not respect the deepest convictions of one or both sets of commitments. The force of my concerns is perhaps best put in the form of a comparison: Does Harry Ward (1873–1966) (the key early leader in the

---

14. Teasdale has recently shown, for example, that early American Methodist preachers actively sought to convert people not only to faith in Jesus Christ, but to membership in the Methodist Episcopal Church, which suggests a very different environment from Albert Outler and subsequent Methodists' emphasis on ecumenism. See *Methodist Evangelism, American Salvation*.

15. B. T. Roberts's expulsion from the MEC is discussed in further detail in the section "The Gradual Dissolution of a Theological Tradition" of this chapter.

16. This concern is understandable given Vickers's aims in his essay and that he is first and foremost a theologian. I would be interested to hear Vickers describe how this typology can account for the degree of fragmentation within American Methodism. Given the extent of doctrinal disagreement involved, are the many groups that have left (or were expelled from) the broad branch of American Methodism not legitimately American Methodist? Or are they speaking the same language without being aware that they are? Or, how else should we account for these divisions?

Methodist Federation for Social Action) have more in common with Walter Rauschenbusch (1861–1918) (the father of the Social Gospel, who was Baptist) or with Henry Clay Morrison (1857–1942) (the founder of Asbury Theological Seminary in Wilmore, KY, who was Methodist)?

The remainder of this essay seeks to provide an historical narrative of American Methodism as a theological tradition that pays attention to disagreements and fragmentation within American Methodism, resisting the temptation to smooth them over in order to find consistency and coherence. This essay will argue that there was a recognizable theological tradition in American Methodism until about the middle of the nineteenth century, when American Methodism began experiencing major fragmentation and internal challenges. At that time, contemporaries often disagreed with each other about various aspects of what it meant to be a Methodist. Such disagreements were not resolved through the translation of ideas. Rather, people understood each other and thought each other's ideas were damaging, sometimes even to the point of believing that they threatened the core of the Methodist theological heritage itself. Because of the scope of this essay and the necessary limits on length, I will have to paint with much broader brushstrokes than I would prefer. There are many ways the argument could be nuanced, problematized, or reframed. A major goal in this chapter is to urge the necessity of a more focused conversation about American Methodism's theological heritage, taking more seriously on their own terms what the women and men in this history thought was at stake.

Wesley and British Methodism

From the beginning, American Methodists self-consciously built on the work of John Wesley and British Methodism. The first generation of American Methodist leadership was itself British. The details of John Wesley's decision to ordain Richard Whatcoat (1736–1806) and Thomas Vasey (c. 1746–1826) and then Thomas Coke (1747–1816) as "Superintendent," with instructions to ordain Francis Asbury (1745–1816) on their arrival in America are well known.[17] When Wesley took the unprecedented step of providing ordained leadership for Methodists in America by his own authority, he also included liturgy in *The Sunday Service for the Methodists in North America*, a hymnbook in *A Collection of Psalms and Hymns for the*

---

17. See, for example, Richey, Rowe, and Schmidt, *The Methodist Experience in America*, 1: chapters three and four and Wigger, *American Saint*, chap. 8.

Lord's Day, a revision of the Articles of Religion and his own *Sermons* and *Notes*.

After several turbulent years, Methodism in America was formally constituted as a church. Asbury astutely called for a vote of the preachers in America on Wesley's plan, which was approved at the "Christmas Conference" of 1784 in Baltimore, Maryland. Thus, the Methodist Episcopal Church (MEC) was born. What would Wesley have seen to be the essentials of the new church that was largely his creation? For Wesley, there were both essential doctrines and disciplines or practices that were crucial for maintaining the spiritual vitality of Methodism.[18]

Wesley summarized the doctrinal core of Methodism in slightly different ways in different places.[19] In 1746, he gave a fairly concise statement in "The Principles of a Methodist Farther Explained," as already noted in Campbell's essay herein. Wesley wrote, "Our main doctrines, which include all the rest, are three, that of repentance, of faith, and of holiness. The first of these we account, as it were, the porch of religion; the next, the door; the third is religion itself."[20] Wesley believed in original sin, the need for repentance, justification by faith, the new birth, and ongoing growth in holiness. A major point of emphasis–and controversy–in Wesley's theology was the possibility of holiness in this life. Wesley articulated a theology of entire sanctification or Christian perfection, which he defined in the sermon "The Scripture Way of Salvation" as "love excluding sin."[21]

A major part of Wesley's genius was his ability to organize people together in order to bring doctrine to life in individual experience. The key pieces of Wesleyan discipline were the "General Rules," the class meeting, and the band meeting. These provided the structure that enabled a pursuit of "social holiness" where Methodists pursued holiness together rather than in isolation.[22] The "General Rules" provided a basic template for Methodist practice. Methodists were expected to "do no harm," "do good," and "attend

---

18. See, for example, Wesley, "Thoughts upon Methodism," 527–30.

19. This is one of the places where the scope of this essay does not allow for the kind of nuance that is ideal. There are a variety of places where Wesley provides different summaries of key doctrines. For a thorough treatment of Wesleyan doctrine, see Campbell, *Wesleyan Beliefs*, and his chapter in this volume.

20. Wesley, "The Principles of a Methodist Farther Explained," 227.

21. Wesley, "The Scripture Way of Salvation," 160.

22. On Wesley's understanding of social holiness and the way it was implemented in the band meeting, see Watson, *Pursuing Social Holiness*.

upon the ordinances of God" (that is, practice the means of grace).[23] Methodists were divided into class meetings, which typically had about seven to twelve people in them. These groups were the basic mark of membership in early Methodism, and in them members were held accountable to the "General Rules" and learned to speak of their experience of God, as the class leader was to ask each member how their souls prospered.[24] The band meeting was a smaller group that was voluntary and stratified according to gender and marital status. Bands were particularly focused on the pursuit of holiness. Members confessed sin to one another and encouraged each other to continue growing in holiness.[25]

Though far more could be said about Wesley's doctrinal and disciplinary commitments, the preceding provides the basic foundation of what Wesley saw as essential to Methodism avoiding becoming a "dead sect, having the form of religion without the power."[26] For Wesley, there were doctrinal and disciplinary boundaries that helped one to have clarity about who was and who was not a Methodist. For example, a Methodist was one who attended a weekly class meeting. Failure to attend more than four times in a quarter led to being removed not only from the class meeting but from membership in the Methodist society itself. These boundaries were seen to be necessary to Methodism's vitality.

The Context of American Methodism

While American Methodism was deeply influenced by John Wesley and its British forbearers, it also arose within a markedly different context. The story of American Methodism has been told with the most vivid detail in the period from its beginnings through Francis Asbury's death.[27] The careful attention that has been paid to the beginnings of American Methodism

23. Wesley, "The Nature, Design, and General Rules of the United Societies," 67–75.

24. Ibid., 70. On the early Methodist class meeting, see Watson, *The Early Methodist Class Meeting*.

25. Wesley, "Rules of the Band Societies," 77–78. See also Wesley, "Directions Given to the Band Societies," 79.

26. Wesley, "Thoughts upon Methodism," 527.

27. Notable examples are: Richey, *Early American Methodism*; Wigger, *American Saint* and *Taking Heaven by Storm*; Andrews, *The Methodists and Revolutionary America, 1760-1800*; and Ruth, *A Little Heaven Below*. The recent attention given to American Methodism by scholars was long overdue, as Hatch pointed out in "The Puzzle of American Methodism," 25–27.

can be explained, at least in part, by the astonishing growth of the people called Methodists after the American colonies secured their independence from England. From 1776 to 1850 American Methodism grew from 4,921 members to 2.6 million members, marking one of the most rapid periods of growth in Christian history.[28]

Almost as soon as Methodism was converted from a renewal movement within the Church of England into a church in its own right with the formation of the Methodist Episcopal Church in 1784, American Methodists wrestled with the extent of authority that should be given to John Wesley. At the 1784 Conference, American Methodists initially professed loyalty to Wesley, recognizing that they were Wesley's "Sons in the Gospel, ready in matters belonging to church-government, to obey his commands."[29] But tensions were apparent almost immediately. When Wesley sent clear instructions on church government to the MEC in 1787, all of his instructions were ultimately ignored. Furthermore, the promise to obey Wesley's commands was itself removed from the minutes of that conference.[30]

American Methodism's distancing itself from John Wesley could be seen as an initial expression of the particularities of the American context—as one expression of the "democratization of American Christianity."[31] Yet, one of the ironies of Methodism in America is that as the movement asserted its independence from John Wesley, Francis Asbury increasingly came to play a role in American Methodism that was similar to Wesley's influence in early British Methodism. In fact, Asbury established himself as the recognized leader of American Methodism, in part, by asserting himself as Wesley's equal, particularly concerning matters related to the Methodist Episcopal Church. Wesley seems to have been aware of (and frustrated by) Asbury's desire for equality. Wesley wrote in a 1789 letter of an apparent conversation between Francis Asbury and George Shadford, where Asbury

---

28. Finke and Stark, *The Churching of America, 1776–2005*, 29 and 57.

29. Lee, *A Short History of the Methodists*, 95.

30. Ibid., 126–27. A few decades ago, Heitzenrater uncovered a further expression of American independence when the MEC debated the role of Wesley's *Sermons* and *Notes* and determined that they did not have the same authority as the "Articles of Religion" in the Methodist Episcopal Church. Heitzenrater wrote that the 1808 conference "did not want to specify its Wesleyan measures for orthodoxy beyond the Articles, but it also did not want the public to know that it had been unwilling to go on record in that matter" (see Heitzenrater, "At Full Liberty," 200).

31. This phrase was coined by Hatch and is the title of his book, *The Democratization of American Christianity*.

allegedly said, "Mr. Wesley and I are like Caesar and Pompey: he will bear no equal, and I will bear no superior."[32]

Historian Nathan O. Hatch has noted that, despite the ways in which Methodists in America qualified their allegiance to Wesley, certain emphases of Wesley's thought were received with particular enthusiasm by Methodist preachers and their audiences. Hatch particularly focused on American Methodism's embrace of "God's free grace, the liberty of people to accept or reject that grace, and the power and validity of popular religious expression."[33] One of the broad factors that facilitated American Methodism's rapid growth was the appeal of its message to its native context and its ability to distinguish itself from competitors in the rapidly developing religious marketplace of American religion. Thus, Methodism was compelling because it "transcended class barriers and empowered common people to make religion their own."[34] It was also clearly different from the main competitor on the landscape of American revivalism—Calvinism: In contrast to Calvinism, "Methodists proclaimed the breathtaking message of individual freedom, autonomy, responsibility, and achievement."[35]

Early American Methodist Commitment to Wesley's Doctrine and Discipline

American Methodism thrived in the early republic in large part because of the correspondence of its message with its unique context. Though the context was different than that of British Methodism, the message and method of American Methodists for the first several decades of its existence were both quite consistent with what Wesley had articulated and implemented in Britain. Francis Asbury, in particular, expressed a strong commitment to sustaining both Wesley's core theological commitments as well as his method of organizing the movement. On his voyage to America, Asbury recorded his commitment to Wesleyan-Methodist doctrine and discipline: "The people God owns in England, are the Methodists. The doctrines they preach, and the discipline they enforce, are, I believe, the purest of any

---

32. Wesley's letter also shows that he was aware that his name had been removed from the *Minutes* of the Methodist Episcopal Church. See Wesley, "Letter to Mr. ---, 31 October 1789," 183.

33. Hatch, "The Puzzle of American Methodism," 27.

34. Ibid., 28.

35. Ibid.

people now in the world. The Lord has greatly blessed these doctrines and this discipline in the three kingdoms: they must therefore be pleasing to him."[36]

Despite significant internal tensions in the first decade of the MEC, Asbury and the broader church were united around these initial doctrinal and disciplinary essentials. In the 1798 annotation of *The Doctrines and Discipline of the Methodist Episcopal Church in America*, the doctrines of holiness and entire sanctification feature prominently, as do the "General Rules," the class meeting, and the band meeting. In the section on preaching, *The Doctrines and Discipline* exhorts preachers to "strongly and closely insist upon inward and outward holiness in all its branches."[37] The notes after the section "On Dress" begin by stating that "our one aim, in all our economy and ministerial labours, is to raise *a holy people*."[38] *The Doctrines and Discipline* conclude with a section "On Perfection," which begins, "Let us strongly and explicitly exhort all believers to go on to perfection."[39] Methodists continued to exhort people to grow in holiness and toward perfect love for God and neighbor throughout the first decades of the MEC.

The discipline that Wesley viewed as essential to Methodist vitality was also adhered to by the MEC at both macro (general conferences, annual conferences, quarterly conferences, and circuits and itinerating preachers who constantly travelled circuits of local societies) and micro levels (class leaders and mandatory class meetings for all members, quarterly meetings, and love feasts). These two levels of organization were brought together at camp meetings where circuit-riding preachers would come together and preach week-long revivals to tens of thousands of people.

A commitment to Methodist discipline is also evident in the 1798 *Doctrines and Discipline*. Therein are sections on the "General Rules" as well as on the class meeting and the band meeting. Coke and Asbury's notes on these sections illustrate the way in which doctrine and discipline were connected for early American Methodists. "Section XIII" names the class meeting and the band meeting as prudential means of grace for

---

36. Asbury, Journal Entry, "12 September 1771," 1:4.

37. *The Doctrines and Discipline of the Methodist Episcopal Church in America: With Explanatory Notes, by Thomas Coke and Francis Asbury*, 85.

38. Ibid., 159; emphasis in original.

39. Ibid., 184. The notes refer the reader to "Mr. Wesley's excellent treatise on that subject."

Methodists.[40] The bishops' notes after the section on the band meeting begin by describing Methodist societies as "a spiritual hospital" where people were particularly likely to experience spiritual healing through the classes and bands. The bands were seen to be of particular value because people's hearts were "a cage of unclean birds," making it particularly difficult (and all the more necessary) for people to have a place where they could be completely honest with one another. Thus, Coke and Asbury describe the band meeting as "one of the most profitable means of grace in the whole compass of christian [sic] discipline."[41] They further affirmed that Methodist discipline, "under the grace of God, tends to raise the members of our society from one degree of grace to another."[42]

Throughout Francis Asbury's ministry in America, John Wesley's core doctrine and discipline were brought into the religious marketplace in American culture and were mostly found to be ideally suited for such a context. As a result, the MEC experienced astonishing numerical growth from its creation through the antebellum period. There were conflicts and tensions during this period, but when there was division or a lack of unity, it was not primarily related to doctrinal or disciplinary disagreement.

The key reasons for conflict in the first decades of the MEC were typically related to concerns over the power of the episcopacy and tensions related to race, slavery, and segregation. In 1792, James O'Kelly (1735–1826) left the MEC and formed the Republican Methodist Church. O'Kelly separated from the MEC because of increasing conflict with Asbury's vision of Methodism and related concerns about Asbury's power. The final breaking point came when O'Kelly's motion for preachers to have the right to appeal an appointment made by Asbury was voted down by General Conference. It is significant that O'Kelly's separation was not due to disagreement about the doctrine or discipline of the MEC at the time.[43]

The African Methodist Episcopal Church (AME) was formally constituted as a denomination in 1816 as the result of white racism and moves to segregate MEC churches in Philadelphia and Baltimore. Richard Allen (1760–1831), Absalom Jones (1746–1818), Daniel Coker (1780–1846), and

---

40. Ibid., 92.
41. Ibid., 151.
42. Ibid., 152.
43. See Kilgore, "The James O'Kelly Schism in the Methodist Episcopal Church," esp. 57–58, on the importance of holiness; on O'Kelly's agreement with the doctrine of Christian perfection, see 69.

other black Methodists did not form a new denomination because they disagreed with the importance of holiness or a disciplined commitment to following the "General Rules" and mandatory attendance at a weekly class meeting. Indeed, when Allen later recounted the events that led to separation from the MEC and the formation of the AME, he explicitly noted his ongoing affirmation of MEC doctrine and discipline. Allen recounted that, despite having "been so violently persecuted by the elder [at St. George MEC], we [Allen and Jones] were in favor of being attached to the Methodist connection."[44] Allen continued to value Methodism because Methodists were successful in "the awakening and conversion of the colored people," which he attributed to "plain doctrine and having a good discipline."[45]

James O'Kelly and Richard Allen, who separated from the MEC for different reasons, nevertheless, represent the extent of agreement on the essentials of early American Methodist doctrine and discipline. O'Kelly and Allen both agreed on the importance of holiness for the Christian life. And both men also supported the basic practice of mandatory weekly class meetings. If anything, Allen lamented changes in the early discipline, noting his regret that "the discipline is altered considerably from what it was. We would ask for the good old ways, and desire to walk therein."[46] Thus, the first generation of Methodism in America was marked by a significant agreement about what constituted the essential doctrine and discipline of the "people called Methodists." This broad agreement would hold through the beginning of the nineteenth century.

Constraints in space prevent more than a brief mention of the beginnings of the United Brethren in Christ (UB) and the Evangelical Association (EA), both of which formed independently of the MEC but merged with the Methodist Church (MC) in the twentieth century to form The United Methodist Church (UMC).[47] The UB and EA were initially German speaking and became generally Wesleyan through contact with American Methodists. The key initial leaders of the UB were William Otterbein (1726–1813) (who had been a German Reformed pastor) and Martin Boehm (1725–1812) (previously an Anabaptist pastor). Historians have typically dated the beginning of the UB as a denomination to 1800 when a

---

44. Allen, *The Life, Experience, and Gospel Labors*, 18.
45. Ibid.
46. Ibid., 19.
47. For more on the EA and UB traditions, see O'Malley and Vickers, *Methodist and Pietist*.

number of German preachers met together and decided to meet annually. It has also been widely recognized that this group did not see themselves as forming a denomination. It was not until 1814, for example, that the word *Kirche* (church) was used by them for the first time. Similarly, the beginning of the EA is typically dated to 1807, when regular Annual Conferences were organized and Jacob Albright (1759–1808) (initially a German Lutheran) was elected bishop.

Both groups initially formed class meetings and largely translated the MEC *Doctrines and Discipline* into German. The doctrine and discipline of the UB and EA were similar enough to that of the MEC that historians have often wondered why they remained separate from each other and from the MEC. The UB and EA ultimately would merge with each other in 1946, and the newly constituted Evangelical United Brethren (EUB) would merge with the MC in 1968 to form The UMC. When one looks back to the early 1800s, however, the most obvious difference between these two groups and the MEC is that the UB and EA were German speaking and separated by some significant cultural differences. Once again, there was large agreement on the basic doctrinal and disciplinary essentials that Wesley himself had identified. In fact, when the EUB merged with the MC in 1968 to form The UMC, it was the EUB doctrinal statement that contained the clearest adherence to the Wesleyan understanding of entire sanctification.[48]

From Francis Asbury's death in 1816 until Phoebe Palmer's work promoting the doctrine of entire sanctification in the late 1830s and 1840s, Methodism continued to hold to the essentials first identified by John Wesley. This is not to say that there was a complete lack of tension within American Methodism: As in the previous period, there was also conflict in the first half of the nineteenth century, even to the point of division and the creation of new denominations.

The formation of the African Methodist Episcopal Zion Church (AMEZ) in 1821 developed out of similar encounters with racism and segregation as Richard Allen and others had experienced when they formed the AME. The AMEZ became a distinct denomination under the leadership of James Varick (1750–1827) and Christopher Rush (1777–1873) in New York City after the 1824 MEC General Conference "failed to embrace" the independent African American churches in New York.[49] The AMEZ's

---

48. The EUB statement on "Sanctification and Christian Perfection" can be found in Article XI of "The Confession of Faith of the Evangelical United Brethren Church," in *The Book of Discipline of The United Methodist Church, 2012*, 73.

49. Richey, Rowe, and Schmidt, *The Methodist Experience in America*, 1:145.

commitment to the essentials of early Methodist doctrine and discipline is seen in part in its continued printing of not only the "General Rules" in its *Discipline* but also in its inclusion of sections on the class meeting up to the present.[50]

Similar to the beginning of the Republican Methodist Church in 1792, the Methodist Protestant Church formed in Baltimore in 1830, primarily due to objections to the power of the episcopacy. Methodist Protestants also desired lay representation at annual conferences and General Conference. The efforts to reform the MEC from within were consistently rebuffed throughout the 1820s, eventually leading to the formation of this new denomination.[51] And yet, once again, this group did not represent a major challenge to the doctrine and discipline of early American Methodism. The first article of the "Articles of Association," for example, was explicit in its adherence to both the doctrine and discipline of the MEC, "*Article 1st.* Adopts the Articles of Religion, General Rules, Means of Grace, Moral Discipline, and Rites and Ceremonies in the main of the Methodist Episcopal Church."[52]

The Gradual Dissolution of a Theological Tradition

On May 21, 1835, Sarah Lankford experienced entire sanctification. A group of women soon thereafter met at Lankford's house on Tuesday afternoons. This group became known as the Tuesday Meeting for the Promotion of Holiness. Just over two years later, Lankford's sister, Phoebe Palmer, experienced entire sanctification on July 26, 1837. The Tuesday Meeting, along with Palmer's writing and speaking, brought a new focus to the doctrine of entire sanctification, particularly in Palmer's articulation of a "shorter way," where people entirely consecrated themselves to God, had

---

50. *The Doctrines and Discipline of the African Methodist Episcopal Zion Church*, 2008, 20–22, 25–26, 66–67, and 104–5. The AME *Discipline* also includes the full text of the "Rules of the Band Societies"; see *The Doctrine and Discipline of the African Methodist Episcopal Church*, 2012, 34–38. In contrast to the contemporary UMC, the AMEZ and AME both continue to include sections on the class meeting that suggest that every member should participate in one; see *The Doctrines and Discipline of the African Methodist Episcopal Zion Church*, 2008, 25–26, 66–67, and 104–5 and *The Doctrine and Discipline of the African Methodist Episcopal Church*, 2012, 58 and 68–69.

51. For more on the issues leading to the formation of the MPC, see Strong, "American Methodism in the Nineteenth Century," 70–71.

52. Drinkhouse, *History of Methodist Reform*, 2:211.

faith that God would receive their sacrifice, and then testified to what God had done for them.[53] The Tuesday Meeting was attended by many prominent Methodists, such as Nathan Bangs, Bishop Hamline, and Bishop Janes. When there were disagreements, they tended to be about how to best understand particular aspects of the doctrine (such as the relationship of faith to the witness of the Spirit) and not on whether entire sanctification was a significant doctrine for Methodists. In other words, the value of entire sanctification itself was largely assumed by Methodists during the beginnings of the Holiness Movement.

Phoebe Palmer was not only a vocal advocate of the doctrine of entire sanctification, but she was also actively involved in Methodist class meetings. Ellen Stowe, who would become Ellen Roberts when she and B. T. Roberts were married in 1849, had regular contact with Palmer throughout the 1840s. In 1841 Stowe met with a class meeting that was partly led by Palmer, and she had direct conversation with Palmer about her search for entire sanctification.[54] Entire sanctification and the class meeting, then, both continued to be prominent in New York City Methodism in the 1840s, though both were changing from their original expressions.[55]

Towards the middle of the nineteenth century, the MEC was showing signs of going through significant change. American Methodism had gone from being a small and insignificant group to the largest denomination in the United States on the eve of the Civil War. The dramatic growth of the MEC brought with it equally dramatic embourgeoisement, as Methodist leaders expressed growing concern for the quality of church buildings, parsonages for pastors, and an educated ministry (among other concerns). Peter Cartwright and other Methodist circuit riders sharply criticized the worldliness and compromise they saw taking place at the end of their lives. These concerns were expressed frequently enough that these preachers became known as "croakers," and their laments were classified into their own genre.[56]

---

53. Palmer, *The Way of Holiness*.

54. Snyder, *Populist Saints*, 61 and 76.

55. Snyder points out that Ellen Stowe "never experienced the class meeting the way it was originally designed by Wesley," mostly because they had grown quite large. The size of the classes made sharing with intimacy and depth virtually impossible (*Populist Saints*, 62). On New York City Methodism, see ibid., 54–57.

56. See Wigger, *Taking Heaven by Storm*, 181–88. For an example, see Cartwright, *Autobiography of Peter Cartwright*.

Old circuit riding preachers were not the only ones who worried about Methodism's accommodation to worldliness and the inevitable loss of the power of religion. Some younger Methodists also began to critique their own tradition from within for compromising on a variety of fundamentals. A shift from disputes about polity and church policy to more basic theological disagreements is seen in the events leading to the formation of the Wesleyan Methodist Church (WMC) in 1843. In the decade prior, members of the MEC in New England and New York widely embraced abolitionism, which was distinct from being anti-slavery. Abolitionists argued that slavery was sin, and as sin it must be ended immediately and without compensation to those who held people in bondage.

The 1840 General Conference of the MEC rebuffed the efforts of Orange Scott (1800–1847) and Luther Lee (1800–1889) to convert the MEC to a clear abolitionist position, even issuing a gag order that forbade further discussion of abolition at General Conference, annual conferences, or in denominational publications. When Scott, Lee, and others subsequently formed a new Methodist denomination, they intentionally named it the Wesleyan Methodist Church. In case this was too subtle, their initial publication was named the *True Wesleyan.* Wesleyan Methodists accused the MEC of being "not only a slave holding, but a *slavery defending church*," and so they were no longer sufficiently Wesleyan in their theology and practice.[57]

Just over a decade after the beginnings of the WMC, Benjamin Titus Roberts became so concerned about the compromise and changes in Methodism in western New York state that he wrote an article published in the *Northern Independent* titled "New School Methodism." Roberts worried that "there is springing up among us a class of preachers whose teaching is very different from that of the Fathers of Methodism." Roberts then outlined the differences that he saw between "Old School" and "New School" Methodists. He pointed to differences in understanding the relationship between justification and entire sanctification and the meaning of holiness itself. He also pointed to departing understandings of Methodist discipline, as there were deep disagreements about the means of grace and the necessity of the class meeting.[58]

In a passage that challenges more recent historiography related to a broad American Methodist theological tradition, Roberts is explicit that

---

57. Scott, "The Grounds of Secession from the M. E. Church," 257; italics in original.
58. See the extended quoted material in Snyder, *Populist Saints*, 389–92.

the Genesee Conference of the MEC was deeply divided and was practicing two incompatible religions: "Two distinct parties exist. With the one or the other every preacher is in sympathy. This difference is fundamental. It does not relate to things indifferent, but to those of the most vital importance. It involves nothing less than the nature itself of Christianity."[59] Roberts's concerns were explicitly tied to social concerns and his understanding of what holiness looked like in practice. Believing that bad theology corrupted early Methodist practice, Roberts wrote that "Old School Methodists rely . . . upon the agency of the Holy Ghost, and the purity of the Church. The New School Methodists appear to depend upon the patronage of the worldly, the favor of the proud and aspiring; and the various artifices of worldly policy."[60] For Roberts, "Old" and "New School" Methodism were incompatible. He believed that the "New School" would lead to the destruction of Methodism itself. Methodists in the Genesee Conference of the MEC could either maintain the old doctrine and discipline and "continue to be favored of Heaven, and the joy of the earth," or they could:

> receive to her communion all those lovers of pleasure, and lovers of the world, who are willing to pay for the privilege . . . and [as a result] Methodism will become a dead and corrupting body, endeavoring in vain to supply, by the erection of splendid churches, and the imposing performances of powerless ceremonies, the manifested glory of the Divine presence, which once shone so brightly in all her sanctuaries.[61]

The "New School" Methodists disagreed with B. T. Roberts about many things. But they agreed with him that their vision for Methodism was incompatible with his. On September 2, 1857, less than a week after the second part of "New School Methodism" was published, charges were brought against B. T. Roberts at the Genesee Annual Conference by Reuben Foote, accusing Roberts of "unchristian and immoral conduct."[62] The charges listed nine parts of Roberts's article that were the most offensive. The Conference ultimately found Roberts guilty by a vote of 52 to 43. Among other things, the vote showed that Roberts was correct—the Conference was in fact deeply divided! The following year, when George Estes republished Roberts's piece in a broader pamphlet, Estes wrote against the "New School"

---

59. As quoted in ibid., 389–90.
60. As quoted in ibid., 383.
61. As quoted in ibid., 395.
62. Ibid., 401.

Methodists, and Roberts was himself again tried for "unchristian and immoral conduct." He was again convicted, this time by a vote of 62 to 32. The conference then voted to expel Roberts from the Genesee Conference.

B. T. Roberts's trials and expulsion from the Genesee Conference of the MEC ultimately led to the formation of the Free Methodist Church (FMC), founded in 1860. The events in 1857 and 1858 in the Genesee Conference demonstrate that a significant change was taking place in American Methodist theology and practice. In his biography of B. T. and Ellen Roberts, historian Howard A. Snyder argued that Roberts's "main concern in 'New School Methodism' is the drift away from historic Methodism in both doctrine and practice."[63] Was a Methodist still fundamentally someone who was pursuing "holiness of heart and life?"[64] Were Methodists still convinced that particular practices were indispensable to this end? B. T. Roberts's expulsion from the MEC for pressing on these points demonstrates that a significant shift in American Methodism was well underway.

As understandings of holiness and entire sanctification shifted in American Methodist theology, so did understandings of holy living. In the Preface to *Why Another Sect*, Roberts laid particular emphasis on the practices that came from a commitment to entire sanctification. In what is doubtless intended as a contrast to the MEC, Roberts described the Free Methodist Church's commitment to not only having some free seats "but that all the seats be free."[65] The mission of the FMC, according to Roberts, was "to uphold the New Testament standard of religion; and to preach the Gospel to the poor."[66] When MEC bishop Matthew Simpson (1811–1884) delivered an address at the Centenary of American Methodism, his emphasis was notably different. Reflecting his desire for a respectable Methodism, Simpson directed his audience to "look at our commodious churches, our large congregations, the wealth, the influence, the refinement, the great enterprise, and we see that a mighty work has been accomplished, and we can well exclaim, 'What hath God wrought!'"[67] As Simpson peered into the future, he saw a Methodism that would be more passionate about Methodists securing their rightful place at the upper levels of American society

---

63. Ibid., 384.

64. Wesley, "The Character of a Methodist," 35. This phrase was one Wesley commonly used and can be found in many places in his writings.

65. Roberts, *Why Another Sect*, viii.

66. Ibid.

67. Simpson, "The Centenary of American Methodism," 505.

than American Methodism's first mission to "spread scripture holiness." Simpson saw, and was enthusiastic about the prospect of, "a people vast in number . . . with intellects educated, with tastes refined, artistic, lovely, energetic, and expressive—going forth preaching the Gospel in all languages, and conquering the world unto God."[68]

Increasing Fragmentation of American Methodist Theology

The Holiness Movement continued to grow and gain momentum in the decades after the formation of the Free Methodist Church. In many parts of the main branch of Methodism, key leaders passionately embraced and proclaimed the holiness message. There were also increasingly those who resisted the emphasis on holiness, particularly its less than dignified or refined expressions. The extent to which Methodism was moving simultaneously in different directions can be seen in the divergent visions of figures who were contemporaries. In the late nineteenth and early twentieth centuries these competing visions for American Methodism are exemplified within two pairings: Phineas Bresee (1838–1915) and John Heyl Vincent (1832–1920) in California Methodism and Borden Parker Bowne (1847–1910) and Henry Clay Morrison (1857–1942) in Methodist theological education.

Phineas F. Bresee began preaching in Iowa and had been an effective preacher there for twenty-five years. While pastoring in Chariton, IA, in the mid-1860s, Bresee had an experience that he later described as receiving "the baptism with the Holy Ghost" or entire sanctification.[69] Bresee moved to California in 1883, and during his ministry there, he increasingly embraced and emphasized holiness in his preaching. His proclamation of entire sanctification ran parallel to his rising influence in the Southern California Annual Conference. Bresee served as a trustee for the University of Southern California (an MEC institution), and in 1891 he was appointed presiding elder of the Los Angeles District by Bishop Mallalieu, an ally of

---

68. Ibid., 512. This is an excellent example of what Mark Teasdale has recently described as "pure American evangelism," where the evangelistic message of the MEC came to be at least as concerned with spreading the values of white middle-class American Methodists as it was with "spreading scriptural holiness." See Teasdale, *Methodist Evangelism, American Salvation*, 36.

69. Bangs, *Phineas F. Bresee*, 72.

the Holiness Movement. In 1891, Bresee was also the first clergy delegate elected to attend the 1892 General Conference.

As Bresee rose in prominence in California Methodism and his commitment to preaching holiness deepened, the holiness message was also increasingly resisted by other key leaders in the Conference. The most entrenched resistance perhaps came from John Heyl Vincent, who was elected to the episcopacy in 1888 and presided at annual conference in 1892. Vincent was passionately committed to the importance of religious education for the Christian life, emphasizing life-long learning and intellectual understanding of the Christian faith over both crisis moments of conversion and deep personal experience of salvation by faith.

Vincent also opposed Bresee's passionate advocacy of revivalism and Bresee's call for an experience of entire sanctification as a kind of second conversion experience because they ran counter to his emphasis on ongoing Christian education. Prior to being elected to the episcopacy in 1888, Vincent had led the Sunday School Union (SSU) for twenty years. Under Vincent's leadership, the SSU saw incredible growth. The SSU grew by ten thousand Sunday schools with a total of 278,000 teachers and more than one million students in the MEC.[70] According to one interpreter, "two themes dominated Vincent's life—self-education and a distaste for revivalism."[71] Vincent's dislike of revivalism sometimes came through even when he tried to counter the accusation that he was opposed to revivals. In his autobiography, for example, he wrote, "*I am not opposed to revivals.* But I am opposed to all superficiality, and spasmodic effort as a substitute for calm, rational, intelligent, unremitting endeavor for twelve months every year."[72]

As a result, Vincent was hostile to the holiness camp meetings that Bresee and others supported. Vincent used his authority to mute Bresee's message of holiness and his powerful public presence at annual conference by asking all presiding elders to submit written reports to the conference, rather than addressing the conference in person. Vincent subsequently appointed Bresee to Simpson Church, a large church that faced the prospect of financial ruin and whose membership was largely opposed to Bresee's holiness message.

---

70. Kirby, Richey, and Rowe, *The Methodists*, 204.

71. Ibid.

72. Vincent, "The Autobiography of Bishop Vincent," 846.

After serving for one year at Simpson Church, Bresee asked to be appointed to Peniel Mission, a ministry to the poor of Los Angeles and a hub for holiness adherents in the area. On learning that a regular appointment was impossible, he requested a supernumerary relation to the conference. This was ultimately tabled, in part because supernumerary status was conceived as a "temporary exemption from traveling ministry because of ill health," for which Bresee did not qualify, nor claim to qualify.[73] "After a night of prayer and thought," Bresee decided to locate, which meant that he was no longer part of the traveling ministry or membership of the annual conference.[74] This move was the initial step that led to Bresee ultimately becoming the key leader of the Church of the Nazarene.

Vincent was most passionate about Christian education and a lifetime of Christian nurture. Bresee was most passionate about revivalistic preaching and the call for and experience of entire sanctification. These two men did not entirely disagree with each other. Bresee valued education and Vincent, at least for a period of time in his work for the SSU, had conversion as a goal of Sunday school curriculum.[75] The divergence is seen in where they placed their primary emphasis and in Vincent's opposition to revivalism. Vincent and Bresee's differences led to competing visions within the MEC.

If Bresee and Vincent show fragmentation of American Methodism in a particular geographical area of Methodism at the end of the nineteenth century, Borden Parker Bowne and Henry Clay Morrison illustrate increasing fragmentation within theological education in American Methodism.[76] As American Methodists increasingly sought to become visible players in the world of theological education, a vision for American Methodist theology was articulated that was increasingly a departure from American Methodism's Wesleyan beginnings.

The work of Borden Parker Bowne largely increased Methodism's visibility in the world of education. Bowne was raised by devout Methodists. Bowne's mother, Margaret, was deeply influenced by Phoebe Palmer and the early Holiness Movement. Bowne's father, Joseph, was a local preacher who pursued personal holiness as well; he was also against slavery and alcohol. After graduating as valedictorian of New York University in 1871,

---

73. Bangs, *Phineas F. Bresee*, 188.

74. Girvin, *Phineas Bresee*, 101.

75. Kirby, Richey, and Rowe, *The Methodists*, 204.

76. Strong develops this comparison in "Borden Parker Bowne and Henry Clay Morrison," 297–306.

Bowne went to Göttingen for graduate work. In Germany, Bowne studied with Rudolf Hermann Lotze (1817–1881), a post-Hegelian idealist whose thinking had a profound influence on Bowne. Lotze believed that "personality is the ultimate reality and that the existence and teleological agency of a personal deity in history is disclosed to human agents principally through feeling."[77] Without completing a doctorate, Bowne was offered the chair of the philosophy department at Boston University in 1876. Bowne occupied this position for thirty-five years. During these decades, Bowne's personalist philosophy became a highly influential school that not only increased Boston University's reputation but also had a significant impact on American Methodist theological education.

As a result, there is perhaps no better figure to exemplify the shifts in American Methodist theology in the late nineteenth and early twentieth century than Borden Parker Bowne. Bringing Bowne into the conversation of American Methodism as a theological tradition is also difficult because he did not appear himself to be intentionally developing that tradition as much as he was seeking to be a leading voice in contemporary philosophy. Bowne, for example, rarely talked about John Wesley in his own work.

Nevertheless, Francis J. McConnell makes several connections in his biography of Bowne. McConnell, who was a student of Bowne's and later a bishop of the MEC, was aware of the role of the witness of the Spirit and assurance in the Wesleyan tradition, as he wrote that "the Methodist Episcopal Church began with an emphasis on inner experience in the heart of the Christian . . . they taught that a man might know inwardly that he was saved by a witness of the Spirit."[78] However, in Bowne's time this had come to be "almost a standardized experience."[79] And by the time McConnell wrote his biography of Bowne, he commented that "the present generation does not know much about that former teaching of old-time Methodism, but we are more and more hearing an emphasis on mysticism which is just as perplexing and baffling."[80]

McConnell then summarized a concern that both he and Bowne seemed burdened to address: the role of personal experience as justification in Christian theology. McConnell remarks,

---

77. Dorrien, *The Making of American Liberal Theology*, 373.

78. McConnell, *Borden Parker Bowne*, 207.

79. Ibid. This is an interesting criticism, given how at the same time the shift from conversion to nurture was equally standardized.

80. Ibid.

> The Methodist Episcopal Church used to suffer intensely from the religious arrogance—I might almost say bulldozing—of those who, on the basis of 'experiences,' claimed spiritual authority to tell others how to live, or gave themselves to courses annoying to others, expecting those others to acquiesce without complaint. Sometimes these enlightened souls were church officials, sometimes ministers, sometimes laymen, and at all times Bowne considered them nuisances.[81]

Bowne's solution to this problem resulted in a departure from prior Methodist theology. According to McConnell, Bowne "laid stress on the righteous will as the center of Christian experience."[82] Bowne did not entirely rule out "mystical experiences," but he considered them "supernormal."[83] For Bowne, direct encounters with God were suspect and not essential; rather, what was essential was "the will firmly set to do the purpose of God, and to find that purpose if it had to be sought for."[84] For decades before Bowne, American Methodists had seen the experience of finding peace with God through the witness of the Spirit as the most certain knowledge one can have of the forgiveness of one's sins and of one's status as a child of God. Bowne, on the other hand, attributed "most of what used to pass as 'finding peace' in religion . . . to psychological rhythm, or the swing of nervous periodicity."[85] For Bowne, "the escape from the consequences of sin could be achieved, not by any word of forgiveness, but by the actual working of the will toward righteousness."[86] In other words, the solution to the problem of sin was not repentance and justifying faith, followed by holiness, as it had been for Wesley; the solution came through individuals applying their will and working toward righteousness. As a result of Bowne's optimism of natural human ability, Bowne preferred to focus on the "bringing in of the Kingdom through persuading men to yield their wills to the divine will" rather than through "evangelistic methods as ordinarily practiced."[87] The sense of discord between Bowne and some in Methodism at the time is

81. Ibid., 211.
82. Ibid., 209.
83. Ibid., 210.
84. Ibid.
85. Ibid., 211.
86. Ibid., 221.
87. Ibid., 222.

highlighted by the fact that he was formally tried for heresy in 1904, though he was not convicted.[88]

As the mainstream of Methodism in America increasingly turned toward nurture and education and away from what had been distinctive marks of Methodist doctrine and discipline (repentance, faith and holiness, and the class meeting), there were those who stayed within the MEC and resisted what they viewed as a departure from the Methodist theological tradition. Henry Clay Morrison, a contemporary of Bowne's, reacted against Boston Personalism and the destructive impact that the mainstream of theological education in Methodism was having on Methodist pastors and congregations. Morrison emphasized key doctrines that he believed were central to vital Christianity. Among these were the inspiration of the Scriptures, the reality of sin, the deity of Jesus, and belief in the miraculous. Morrison further argued for the importance of revival and a life committed to holiness. By the 1920s, Morrison had concluded that Methodist schools such as Boston University were no longer capable of adequately preparing people for Christian ministry. As a result, Morrison founded a new seminary: Asbury Theological Seminary in Wilmore, Kentucky.[89]

Douglas M. Strong has recently compared the strikingly different conceptions of Methodism found in Bowne and Morrison, noting the divergence in their understanding of experience and its significance for the Christian life:

> More than perhaps anyone else, Bowne helped to clarify the thinking of Methodists as to the role of religious experience, altering it from the witness of the Spirit regarding Christ's saving work on the cross to an apprehension of God's divine will in one's life. Other Methodists, such as Morrison, hoped to retain the conventional Wesleyan understanding of Christian "affections" as an assurance of faith. These two belief systems, and their corresponding social locations, created a dual approach to Methodism that lasted for most of the twentieth century.[90]

Though Morrison did not leave the branch of Methodism that he was reared in, many Methodists did choose to leave the MEC and MECS because of their convictions that the MEC and MECS had abandoned their heritage.

---

88. See Richey, Rowe, and Schmidt, *The Methodist Experience in America*, 2:460–64.

89. This summary is dependent upon Strong, "Borden Parker Bowne and Henry Clay Morrison," 297–306.

90. Ibid., 306.

Other Methodists, such as B. T. Roberts, were forced to leave because they spoke against what they saw as the captivity of American Methodism to the broader culture and to the pursuit of upward mobility rather than entire sanctification.

In my view, it is difficult to see how Simpson, Vincent, and Bowne on the one hand and Roberts, Bresee, and Morrison on the other represent, in Langford's terms, one "historical stream" with "dominant characteristics" that "conveys an enduring sense of meaning."[91] And, in contrast to Vickers's typology, the disagreements these people had were deeper and more substantive theologically than could be overcome simply by becoming multi-lingual in Wesleyan and liberal languages. The fact that Roberts's colleagues in the Genesee Conference voted to expel him from the conference suggests that they did not see themselves as part of one stream or as different, but nevertheless valid, ways of expressing the same tradition. I am similarly not aware of any evidence that suggests that Bowne and Morrison thought that they were working in the same direction with different points of emphasis. A more candid assessment is that they saw the other's message as a threat to the essence of their theological tradition. Readings of American Methodist theology that argue that all the different expressions of American Methodist theology could or should be combined in one articulation of Methodist dogmatic theology do not seem to take people like Roberts, Simpson, Bresee, Vincent, Bowne, and Morrison seriously on their own terms.

Albert C. Outler and the Rediscovery of John Wesley for American Methodist Theology

From Bowne to Albert C. Outler (1908–1989), there was a general lack of intentional study of the roots of American Methodism or its development as a distinctive theological tradition. American Methodism as a theological tradition went into a kind of hibernation as Methodist theological education shifted towards the competing alternatives of mainline liberal Protestantism and conservative holiness evangelicalism. A key shift came when Outler published a collection of John Wesley's writings in Oxford University Press's *Library of Christian Thought*.[92] The success of this vol-

---

91. Langford, *Practical Divinity*, 11.

92. Outler, *John Wesley*. For Outler's own account of this volume and its subsequent influence on Wesleyan studies, see "'A New Future for Wesley Studies'" 132–37. As he

ume led to a full blown critical edition of John Wesley's works, which was an important factor in a renewed interest in Wesleyan studies in The United Methodist Church. Outler's academic work intersected with his ecclesial work, particularly in the events leading to the development of The United Methodist Church and the initial statement "Our Theological Task" in the first UM *Book of Discipline*.

A major challenge for Outler in his ecclesial service to the church was working to provide a way forward when confronted with the bewildering theological diversity that was present from the beginnings of The UMC. In his "Introduction to the Report of the 1968–72 Theological Study Commission," Outler wrote, "Somewhere in The United Methodist Church there is somebody urging every kind of theology still alive and not a few that are dead."[93] Outler recognized the challenge of "theological pluralism" in United Methodism but ultimately viewed it as a positive rather than a negative for the health of The UMC. For Outler, "Far from being a license to doctrinal recklessness or indifferentism, the Wesleyan principle of pluralism holds in dynamic balance both the biblical focus of all Christian doctrine and also the responsible freedom that all Christians must have in their theological reflections and public teaching."[94] The end of this introduction reveals Outler's solution to the challenge of theological pluralism:

> We have tried to open the way for the widest possible participation of United Methodists in the mutual task of the teaching church. Instead of presuming to tell our people what to think, theologically, we have tried to offer basic guidance as to how we may all do theology together, faithful to our rich and yet very diverse heritage, and yet also relevant to our present ideological confusion.[95]

The basic guidance was made concrete in the so-called "Wesleyan Quadrilateral." The Quadrilateral shifted the conversation in Methodism away from particular doctrinal commitments that were unifying to a focus on a method for doing theological reflection. The unity in United Methodist doctrine, then, would not actually be doctrine, but a way of thinking about

---

himself recognized, Outler was by no means the only person responsible for the renewed interest in Wesley in the mid-nineteenth century. Colin Williams, John Deschner, and Frank Baker were three key contributors, among others.

93. Outler, "Introduction to the Report of the 1968–72 Theological Study Commission," 21.

94. Ibid.

95. Ibid., 25.

doctrine. Outler suggested that Wesley added experience, particularly the experience of the witness of the Spirit and assurance, to the Anglican triad of Scripture, tradition, and reason.[96]

Perhaps more than anything else, the Quadrilateral has influenced contemporary Methodist theological reflection and current disagreement about the extent to which American Methodism has meaningful doctrinal consensus or unity. As a result, the Quadrilateral is of particular significance for a study of theological transitions in American Methodism. After the formation of The United Methodist Church in 1968, Outler led the group that wrote "Our Theological Task" that appeared in the 1972 *Book of Discipline* of The United Methodist Church. Despite the fact that this statement was thoroughly revised in 1988, the vision for Methodism that was cast in 1972 has been of lasting influence in United Methodism.

The paragraph from this statement of 1972 that begins the discussion of the four sources of theological reflection that are commonly referred to as the Quadrilateral (Scripture, tradition, reason, and experience) is of particular significance and, as such, is worth quoting in its entirety:

> Since "our present existing and established standards of doctrine" cited in the first two Restrictive Rules of the Constitution of The United Methodist Church are not to be construed literally and juridically, then by what methods can our doctrinal reflection and construction be most fruitful and fulfilling? The answer comes in terms of our free inquiry within the boundaries defined by four main sources and guidelines for Christian theology: Scripture, tradition, experience, reason. These four are interdependent; none can be defined unambiguously. They allow for, indeed they positively encourage, variety in United Methodist theologizing. Jointly, they have provided a broad and stable context for reflection and formulation. Interpreted with appropriate flexibility and self-discipline, they may instruct us as we carry forward our never-ending tasks of theologizing in The United Methodist Church.[97]

Thus, the Quadrilateral was to provide a uniquely United Methodist approach to theology. United Methodist theology would not consist of a

---

96. Much has been written on Outler's conception of the Quadrilateral, as well as Wesley's understanding and use of these four sources. See especially Outler, "The Wesleyan Quadrilateral—In John Wesley"; Campbell, "The 'Wesleyan Quadrilateral'"; Gunter et al., *Wesley and the Quadrilateral*; and Thompson, "Outler's Quadrilateral, Moral Psychology, and Theological Reflection in the Wesleyan Tradition."

97. "Our Theological Task," 75.

commitment to a set of beliefs or doctrinal commitments that were binding or enforceable juridically. The uniqueness of United Methodist theology would not be marked by its theological conclusions; rather, it would be distinct because of a common method that would be used to arrive at conclusions that would inevitably be varied and divergent.

It should be noted that experience was given a particular definition in the 1972 statement of "Our Theological Task." It was defined as "the personal appropriation of God's unmeasured mercy in life and interpersonal relationships."[98] Interestingly, the statement on experience referred both to "personal faith" and "assurance," seeming to define experience analogously to John Wesley's understanding of the witness of the Spirit. The statement continued, "this new relationship of assurance is God's doing, his free gift through the Holy Spirit. This 'new life in Christ' is what is meant by the phrase 'Christian experience.'"[99]

The 1972 statement bore the marks of Outler's work. Assurance and conversion were both key pieces of Outler's description of experience, as would be particularly visible in his 1985 essay on the Wesleyan roots of the Quadrilateral. In that essay, Outler defined experience as "the assurance of one's sins forgiven."[100] He further described Wesley's addition of experience to the Anglican triad of Scripture, tradition, and reason as Wesley's attempt "to incorporate the notion of *conversion* into the Anglican tradition—to make room in it for his own conversions and those of others."[101] He went on to circumscribe the role of experience even more strongly, "Christian experience adds nothing to the substance of Christian truth; its distinctive role is to energize the heart so as to enable the believer to speak and do the truth in love."[102]

To my knowledge, scholars have not explored potential connections between Outler's vision of the Quadrilateral and Boston Personalism.[103] There is good reason to suspect that Outler was not the first Methodist to connect the four sources of the Quadrilateral. Forty years before the 1972

98. Ibid., 77.
99. Ibid.
100. Outler, "The Wesleyan Quadrilateral," 77.
101. Ibid., 79.
102. Ibid., 78.
103. Langford does note that "Knudson insisted that the source and norm of theology . . . is the Bible, and the subordinate sources are Christian tradition, reason, and religious experience." But, he does not connect this to Outler's development of the Quadrilateral. See Langford, *Practical Divinity*, 180.

statement of "Our Theological Task," Albert C. Knudson (1873–1953), Bowne's student and a professor at Boston University, discussed the sources of theological reflection: "We have, then, as definitive of the unique or special field of theology, one main source, the Bible, and particularly the New Testament, and three additional sources which may be described as supplementary or regulative; namely, the church, the natural reason as expressed in the theistic philosophies, and Christian experience."[104] Knudson identified the same four sources as Outler would four decades later. Given the attention that has been given to the Quadrilateral and its ongoing influence in United Methodist consciousness, further investigation of the extent to which (if any) Outler was dependent on Knudson for his conception of the Quadrilateral is needed. One point of departure is that Outler's understanding of experience was remarkably distinct from that of Bowne, Knudson, and the Personalist school. Whereas Bowne and Knudson had no place for conversion, immediate experiences of God's pardoning presence, or confirmation of one's salvation by faith through the witness of the Spirit, Outler seemed to view these as essential to any conception of experience that was faithful to the Wesleyan theological tradition.

Towards the end of his 1985 essay "The Wesleyan Quadrilateral—in John Wesley," Outler himself noted, "the term 'quadrilateral' does not occur in the Wesley corpus—and more than once, I have regretted having coined it for contemporary use, since it has been so widely misconstrued."[105] One explanation for the "misconstrual" of the Quadrilateral may be that Outler was not sufficiently aware of how deeply the popular understanding of "experience" had changed from John Wesley's context to his own. In reading descriptions of experience as a source in Wesleyan theological method, one consistently detects a note of frustration by scholars at the way experience seems to be consistently appealed to: it is usually imprecise, inaccurate, and different from Wesley's appropriation.[106] To put it a bit too neatly for

---

104. Knudson, *The Doctrine of God*, 187.

105. Outler, "The Wesleyan Quadrilateral," 86.

106. Maddox, for example, begins his chapter in *Wesley and the Quadrilateral* ("The Enriching Role of Experience") with a quotation from a letter to the editor of the *United Methodist Reporter*, "I'm tired of having my interpretations of Scripture dismissed simply because they aren't orthodox. Everyone interprets Scripture from his or her experience, study and reason. Are we supposed to turn off our minds and let traditionalists think for us?" Maddox then comments that this is a "representative glimpse of the current debate over the Quadrilateral among United Methodists." Maddox further states that the statement "reflects the tendency of the opposing parties to frame the debate in terms of a stark dichotomy: *either* we think for ourselves by relying on our individual experience and

the purposes of comparison, my sense of the popular use of the Quadrilateral in contemporary United Methodist discourse is that Outler created a typology for United Methodist theological reflection, but the legacy of Boston Personalism had transformed by that time the original Wesleyan meaning of experience. In discussions of the Quadrilateral, people often assume that experience involves a survey of one's own subjective private feelings and outer individual experiences.[107] Moreover, because of Bowne and Knudson's emphasis on the importance of the "personal" above all else, personal experience has come to be seen as the most authoritative source within popular appropriations of the Quadrilateral, despite the explicit and persistent rejection of such uses by Wesleyan scholars.

A significant renewed interest in the Wesleyan tradition occurred on the eve of the formation of The United Methodist Church and continued in the following decades. It is perhaps telling that the focus was on Wesley and the Wesleyan tradition and not as clearly on Methodism itself as a theological tradition. The 1972 and 1988 statements of "Our Theological Task" both revealed a denomination struggling to articulate a coherent theological tradition to which a large enough percentage of its membership would be able to adhere.[108] As a result, Outler sought unity in the retrieval of John Wesley as a theological mentor and in a particular method of theological reflection. It is telling—and concerning—that doctrine was no longer seen to be a source of unity for a *theological* tradition. These moves suggest the possibility that there was not one coherent theological tradition that united

---

reason, or we submit ourselves to tradition. And it uses the words 'reason' and 'experience' as if their meanings are self-evident" (107).

107. The same general argument could be made with reference to Wesley's use and understanding of reason, which assumed a technical knowledge of the basics of logic that cannot be assumed by the average American or the average Methodist today.

108. The 1972 statement acknowledged that "the theological spectrum in The United Methodist Church ranges over all the current mainstream options and a variety of special-interest theologies as well." While the 1988 statement expressed a stronger commitment to doctrinal consensus, it continued to evidence the tension that results from the ongoing theological breadth within the denomination. The 1988 statement tried to provide nuance within this tension by affirming, "While the Church considers its doctrinal affirmations a central feature of its identity and restricts official changes to a constitutional process, the Church encourages serious reflection across the theological spectrum." Later, the statement says: "United Methodists as a diverse people continue to strive for consensus in understanding the gospel." It is telling that doctrinal consensus is something to be sought rather than found in the doctrinal standards of The UMC. See *The Book of Discipline of The United Methodist Church, 1972*, 70; and *The Book of Discipline of The United Methodist Church, 2012*, 78 and 87.

The UMC but that the new denomination was fragmented into multiple competing traditions, some of which were not Methodist in their origins.[109]

Toward a Coherent American Methodist Theological Tradition

The history of American Methodist theology is complicated by the prevalence of multiple competing visions for what it means to be an American Methodist. On numerous occasions, these visions were incompatible enough that they led to separation—at times voluntary and at other times forced. In the twentieth century, with the emphasis on ecumenism, denominations began to reunite or merge. These mergers expressed a more visible unity within the Body of Christ. However, the merger that formed The UMC in 1968 also brought together a wide variety of theological perspectives into one church.[110] In this context, Albert Outler's big tent vision for American Methodism was a heroic attempt to find meaningful unity within the almost overwhelming theological diversity in mid to late twentieth-century American Methodism.

Jason Vickers's recent work could be viewed as an attempt to advance a similar trajectory for American Methodism. Vickers goes beyond Outler's vision by moving away from finding unity in a common method for doing theological reflection. In fact, Vickers's call for the need for the dogmatic development of American Methodism is an important advance over Outler's vision, which turned attention away from the crucial role of doctrine in the life of a community of faith. However, the proposal for a multi-lingual approach to Methodist dogmatics seems to be another attempt to pursue Outler's big tent theological vision for Methodism. A major strength of this approach is that it moves the conversation back to theology, instead of only a method of doing theology, but a weakness is that prescribing a multi-lingual approach leads to a departure from the beginnings of American Methodism as a theological tradition and it seems unlikely to be capable of

---

109. The point here is not that I am certain that The UMC is no longer a coherent theological tradition, but that there is sufficient evidence of deep internal tension to call for a careful examination of the health and viability of The UMC as a theological tradition.

110. Though the EUB and MC came from common theological roots, by the time of this merger the MC had contained a wide variety of theological voices and perspectives that was already straining it. These tensions were heightened with the addition of the EUB, which at that time was more theologically conservative.

producing a dogmatic theology that is distinctively Methodist. Put sharply, when Methodists disagree on a particular matter, a multi-lingual approach would privilege compromise without showing why it is to be preferred. Placing Wesleyanism as merely one of five languages also seems either to demote the theological significance of Wesley's theological vision as a unifying starting point for American Methodist theology or to elevate the significance of the other languages as equally important.[111] This approach seems most problematic regarding liberalism— particularly liberal Protestant theology—since it was not on the scene during the first half-century of American Methodism. All in all, for nearly a century, American Methodists were not willing to compromise on certain core convictions because these were precisely what made Methodism recognizably Methodist.

Vickers's approach is the most substantive proposal currently on offer, and it may in fact be the best way forward. From a historical perspective, however, such an approach is anachronistic. "Old" and "New School" Methodists in the Genesee Conference were offering competing visions for American Methodism, as were John Heyl Vincent and Phineas Bresee, or Borden Parker Bowne and Henry Clay Morrison. They did not think that the way forward was a multi-lingual approach; rather, they felt that the opposing viewpoint was damaging to the Methodist tradition, sometimes even to the future viability of the Christian faith itself. The history of American Methodism offers little reason for optimism that a vision for theological pluralism is the best way forward. Albert Outler tried this approach, with the result of a trivialization of the role of theology in American Methodism, rather than increased clarity about what it means theologically to be a Methodist. Moreover, a big tent vision, by its very nature, necessarily relativizes things that each "language" holds most dear or the degree of disagreement between them.

In recent decades, various metaphors have been suggested for American Methodism as a theological tradition. Is American Methodist theology a stream with many parts that continue to move forward? Is American Methodist theology a conversation that has breadth and diversity that are challenging but also signs of health and vitality that require theologians to

---

111. In a phone conversation with Vickers, he explained to me that one of the reasons for this move was to correct an over-emphasis on John Wesley and a tendency to ignore other key Methodist theologians, such as William Burton Pope. I am in agreement with Vickers here. My concern is that demoting "Wesleyan" to one of five languages that constitutes Methodism goes too far in minimizing the theological foundation of American Methodism.

be able to speak more than one theological language? Both images contain aspects of the truth, particularly in their ability to include a wide range of voices that have in fact been affiliated with American Methodism. And yet, throughout American Methodism's history there have also been times when a more appropriate image would be that of a fork in the road. In discussing slavery, pew rentals, entire sanctification, or the validity and appropriate content of Christian experience (to name only a few of the relevant issues), Methodists thought the tradition could go in a variety of directions theologically, but what it could not do—at least coherently—was turn in two directions at the same time.

A big tent vision for the church has much to commend it. Indeed, John Wesley himself could be seen to provide warrants for such a vision, as Outler himself pointed out. The problem comes when a Christian community attempts to build a tent that is so big that there is no longer a clear commitment to identifiable essentials. A theological tradition that lacks theological commitments that meaningfully unify it is not in any meaningful sense a theological tradition anymore. The deep conviction of this volume is that the best way forward for contemporary American Methodism, and indeed for global Methodism, is to turn toward the riches of catholic Christianity with a recognizably Methodist accent. The essays in this volume are intended to be an initial indication of the promise and potential of such an approach.

3

The Non-Catholicity of a Catholic Spirit

D. Stephen Long

THE WESLEYAN CATHOLIC SPIRIT has not been, perhaps never was, "catholic." Instead, it distills Christianity to its "essence," identifying the minimal doctrinal commitments necessary for Methodists to remain connected to the Christian tradition.[1] Once this minimal doctrinal commitment is identified, all other aspects of Christian faith, including modes of worship, are situated within a realm where each person can "think and let think." Far from providing a catholic spirit, searching for the "essentials" of Christian faith and dividing them from worship and life is a quintessential Protestant endeavor. This essay first identifies a genuine catholic spirit, and then in a second step contrasts it with what Methodism has done to it. In its very identification of a putative "catholic spirit" as a Wesleyan distinctive, Methodism sacrifices catholicity. Although Wesley's sermon "Catholic Spirit" can easily be read to authorize this Protestantizing of a catholic spirit, it is not the best interpretation of his sermon. The third step in the argument suggests how a more robust catholic spirit might be retrieved. Such retrieval requires both analyzing how the affirmation of catholicity leads to its abandonment and finding resources within Methodism for such retrieval.

---

1. In this chapter, when I speak of "Methodism" or "Methodists," I typically am referring to the tradition claimed by United Methodism.

Embodying Wesley's Catholic Spirit

Catholic Spirit as Fullness

A quest for the "essence of Christianity" has always characterized a strain of Protestantism, and Methodism's interpretation of Wesley's catholic spirit fits seamlessly within that strain. Catholicity, as Hans Urs von Balthasar tirelessly argued, is not about minimum essentials but about the fullness of Christian faith. Catholicity implicates diverse regions, eras, and peoples in communion through a recognizable identification of belief and practice in a "symphony" of truth. Because catholicity assumes a "whole" (*holos*) "according to which" (*kata*) diverse spaces and times are in communion, each implicated in the other, Balthasar feared that the search for "essentials" in post-Vatican II ecumenical theology abandoned catholicity, producing a reductive, primarily Protestant, form of Christianity. In a lecture delivered with Karl Barth on Ash Wednesday 1968 for the Swiss *ökumenischen Gesprächskomissionen*, the last public lecture Barth gave before his death, Balthasar expressed his concern. He wrote,

> A word about the Evangelical-Catholic controversy in general is appropriate here. The present ecumenical dialogue, although it is frequently understood as a cooperative search for Christian truth in focus on the mutual Lord, is understood also as a radical reduction to the allegedly "essential," along with the elimination of all dispensable additions which disturb the understanding. It is clear that the Catholic partner will draw the shorter straw under these conditions for the Reformation already lightened the ship of all its alleged "ballast" four hundred fifty years ago, and today, in the face of the events within the Catholic Church, it speaks, not without satisfaction, of a "need to catch up" (*Nachholbedarf*).[2]

Had Balthasar read Wesley's "Catholic Spirit" or followed its confused interpretation within Methodism, he would have questioned how catholic Methodism's catholicity is. Far from being catholic, he would have argued, the question a "catholic spirit" poses and answers in Methodism is essentially Protestant and seeks to reduce Christianity to a bare minimum. Its quest for the essentials in doctrine throws overboard way too much that is necessary to render doctrine intelligible in the first place. Wesley might have agreed with Balthasar. As will be shown below, he explicitly referred to his catholic spirit as a central Reformation principle. However, much has changed since Wesley made his disparaging comments against "popery" in

---

2. Balthasar, *Einheit und Erneuerung der Kirche*, 36; *Convergences*, 109.

his sermon. Wesley's catholic spirit affirmed "liberty of conscience" against political establishment of a particular religion. Roman Catholicism embraced that same principle at Vatican II, but Wesley's catholic spirit took on a life of its own that now works against any possibility of a catholic unity. The Protestantinizing of a "catholic spirit" reduces catholicity to doctrinal essentials and lets loose a simplification of Christianity that turns on those essentials themselves.

The Crisis of Catholicity: Identifying and Losing Catholic Essentials

Balthasar never denied Christianity has a doctrinal core, but he did claim that catholic faith and practice cannot be reduced to it. When it is, Christianity suffers. Once Christianity gets reduced to its doctrinal essentials, a disturbing conclusion results: Inevitably, those essentials themselves get lost. An ancient theological principle correlated doctrine and worship: *lex orandi lex credendi*, the law of prayer (or worship) is the law of belief and vice versa. Wesley himself affirmed this in his sermon, "Catholic Spirit." He stated, "A variety of opinion necessarily implies a variety of practice."[3] Although he argues against a state-enforcement of opinion and practice, he never affirmed this variety. It results from our current sinful condition. If opinion and practice, doctrine and worship are inextricably linked, then doctrine cannot be made "essential" without recognizing it is always already connected to worship and life. To place the former in the realm of "essentials" and the latter in the realm of "think and let think" is to divide what should not be divided. Once they are divided, doctrine loses its purpose. It becomes nothing more than an assertion, a *mere* opinion by which people are policed. Doctrine no longer matters, except to identify who is willing to be on the right side and who is not. Doctrine primarily becomes a matter of submission to authority, whether it entails enforcement of doctrine or lack of doctrine. Once doctrine becomes this, it will rightly be challenged for the simple reason that doctrine no longer matters.

Let me provide a particular example in which this occurred in a United Methodist seminary where I once taught basic Christian doctrine. This example reveals the problem with the Methodist interpretation of a Wesleyan catholic spirit. As a Methodist clergy member and theologian, I taught doctrine assuming The United Methodist Church was in communion with the

---

3. Wesley, "Catholic Spirit," 85.

doctrinal consensus from the ecumenical councils; such consensus, I imagined, was consistent with the Wesleyan catholic spirit. Because the "Articles of Religion" and "Confession of Faith" of The United Methodist Church are consistent with the conciliar decisions of the ecumenical church before its fateful divisions, and because its hymnody, liturgy, sacraments, and practices of discipleship and worship are unintelligible apart from those teachings, The United Methodist Church shares in a catholic spirit capable of identification among divided churches. Whatever reasons exist for the continuing divisions, identifying God such that the core constitutive practices of worship and discipleship make sense was not among them. Or so I thought. An exchange with a seminary student challenged this conviction.

In response to an assignment that asked, "Who is Jesus Christ and what has he done?" one student presented and defended an adoptionist Christology. Although I never graded based on a student's commitment to a catholic spirit, I made a written comment on her essay that an adoptionist Christology was inconsistent with United Methodist doctrine and was liable to create problems for her with a board of ordained ministry.[4] After reading my comment, she was unhappy. She confronted me and challenged my right to make such a judgment. Was I a bishop, or a member of any board of ordained ministry? Was I a member of the judicial council, a committee on investigation, or a properly constituted court of trial? Moreover, she informed me, her theological position was consistent with a recent published statement from a bishop against whom charges had been made and dropped. The jurisdictional committee on investigation looked into the matter and issued an official ruling that nothing the bishop taught violated The United Methodist Church's doctrines. Her position, unlike mine, had the force of ecclesiastical ruling.

She was referring to the following statements from the bishop: "Jesus was not born the Christ. Rather by the confluence of grace with faith he became the Christ, God's beloved in whom God was well pleased" as well as

---

4. I had in mind statements from the United Methodist "Articles of Religion" and "Confession of Faith" such as Article 2 in the former ("The Son, who is the Word of the Father, the very and eternal God, of one substance with the Father, took man's nature in the womb of the blessed Virgin; so that two whole and perfect natures, that is to say, the Godhead and Manhood, were joined together in one person, never to be divided" [*The Book of Discipline of The United Methodist Church, 2012*, 64]) and Article 2 in the latter ("We believe in Jesus Christ, truly God and truly man, in whom the divine and human natures are perfectly and inseparably united. He is the eternal Word made flesh, the only begotten Son of the Father, born of the Virgin Mary by the power of the Holy Spirit" [*The Book of Discipline of The United Methodist Church, 2012*, 71]).

"Jesus was fully human and fully divine. His humanity was given in his conception and birth through the natural processes of procreation. His divinity was derived, given as gift, from his relationship of trust and obedience with God."[5] The bishop's argument was based on a long-standing interpretation of Methodism's catholic spirit. He wrote, "We are a conciliar people, not a creedal or confessional body."[6]

The student's challenge provoked a theological crisis for me because her logic was flawless. I had no official position within Methodism to make any discrimination among the above statements, but those who did had ruled. The bishop and committee who investigated the matter found no cause for a contradiction between these obvious adoptionist Christological statements and official United Methodist doctrine. In so doing, they appeared to think that nothing significant mattered in what a bishop taught and how it related to Methodism's catholic spirit. Adhering to doctrine was considered to be nothing but an antiquated act by misguided "neoliteralists" that worked against Methodism's "conciliar" principle. A catholic spirit now included an adoptionist Christology. This clever student challenged me to be obedient to The United Methodist Church and accept its official rulings. She created a crisis of obedience. If I were to be obedient to Methodism's catholic spirit, I would have to disobey the substance of catholicity.

Responding to a "Catholic Spirit"

More than a decade has passed since this encounter. It still produces a crisis. To this day, I do not know how to respond to her challenge, the events that made it possible, Methodism's odd connection to its official doctrines, and what obedience entails. If such teachings now fit with a Wesleyan "catholic spirit," what could it possibly mean by "catholic"? Nicholas M. Healy, a Roman Catholic theologian, identifies catholicity among churches in terms of devotion to the early ecumenical consensus.[7] But in Methodism, the "conciliar" principle gets interpreted as an alternative to any such confession. Has even this minimal "catholicity" become problematic among Wesleyans? If so, is Methodism a heretical sect with little to no commitment to maintain any catholicity at all? Such a possibility should cause a theological crisis throughout the church, but it has not. I know that Methodism's official

---

5. Sprague, *Affirmations of a Dissenter*, 41 and 46.
6. Ibid., 108.
7. Healy, *Church, World and Christian Life*, 6.

teachings are not heretical, but it is difficult to deny that the use of a "catholic spirit" by the official agencies to interpret Methodism's distinctiveness as non-confessional is. So what is one who cares about the substance of a catholic spirit and is committed to the Methodist and Wesleyan tradition to do?

One option would be to bring charges against bishops and clergy and ensconce the Methodist Church in trials in order to purify not the church but at least those entrusted with its teaching office of rank heresy. The *Book of Discipline* states that church trials should be a "last resort," and I fully agree. Unfortunately, there seems to be little other "resort" available to United Methodists who are concerned about a catholic spirit. We have no means by which to address theological disagreements. Consistent with this option would be to get involved in General Conference, pass resolutions, and try to change the language in the *Discipline* so that it coheres with the substance of a catholic spirit and compel Methodists to comply. Both strategies have been tried, and neither resulted in connecting Methodism to catholicity. Such juridical approaches can only fail, for they treat doctrine as nothing but a political contest. They emphasize the worry about doctrine present among many leaders in Methodism and fail to reunite what has become divorced—doctrine, worship, and life. They do not show why doctrine might matter.

Another option requires more patience, charity, and generosity. It requires affirming a more substantive "catholic spirit" and working proactively to connect the Wesleyan movement to the catholic tradition not only in terms of a minimum of belief but also in terms of essential core practices, showing how the two are implicated in each other. This option, the option of Wesleyan catholicity, requires patience and communication. Patience is necessary since no substantive commitment to a catholic spirit is on the horizon in the foreseeable future. Communication is necessary to show the interrelationships among doctrine, worship, and life, which will require a Wesleyan *ressourcement* that retrieves the catholic tradition as a central resource for Wesleyan Catholicity similar to Wesley's failed attempt to do so in his *Christian Library*. It will be more important that we read the sources Wesley read (or admonished others to read) than that we read him.

Doctrine must be shown to be more than a political contest. To begin on this slow, plodding task, two things are necessary. First, we need a careful analysis as to why a catholic spirit does not pervade the Wesleyan and Methodist movements. Second, we need a more robust theology of a catholic spirit, which begins with Wesley's important sermon but does not use it primarily as a "method" for doing theology. Instead, this theology will be connected to the General Rules, creeds, worship, and Wesley's theological *ressourcement*. The latter is a testimony to Wesley's "catholic spirit" at its best.

Analysis of the Failure of a Catholic Spirit

The difficulty with a Wesleyan "catholic spirit" goes back to Wesley's sermon by that name, but he is not entirely culpable for the confusion it generated. It was written when Methodism was a movement and not a church. Wesley still drew on the rich catholic tradition of Anglicanism for his understanding of catholicity. Once the movement became a church, however, Wesley's sermon lacked the breadth and depth to sustain catholicity. Without that broader catholic practice, his "catholic spirit" was too minimal to constitute a robust catholic tradition, which generated a significant problem Wesley bequeathed to Methodism as a church. It is a problem that has yet to be resolved. The problem is this: Rather than connecting Methodism to a generous, catholic Christianity, Wesley's "catholic spirit" is primarily understood as an "alternative" to other confessional traditions. His "catholic spirit" perpetuates the problem once it became a putative Wesleyan distinctive that marks it off from other churches who are "confessional."

Since its beginning, Methodism has seen fits and starts where it tries to justify itself as a church by claiming some distinctive. Take for example the 1972 General Conference, where Methodism once again created itself anew. The 1972 General Conference established "Our Theological Task" as the hermeneutic lens by which to interpret Methodism's "catholic spirit" and in so doing reinterpreted Wesley's "catholic spirit" in two contradictory directions. First, a "catholic spirit" identified the Wesleyan movement's connection to a "common heritage" with other Christian confessions. And, secondly, a "catholic spirit" identified the Wesleyan movement as an "alternative" to any confessional church. This "alternative to confession" interpretation was heralded as a Wesleyan distinctive. General Conference explicitly appealed to Wesley's "catholic spirit" to legitimate this interpretation and its attendant theological pluralism: "The theological spectrum in The United Methodist Church ranges over all the current mainstream options and a variety of special-interest theologies as well. This is no new thing. Our founders supported what Wesley called 'catholic spirit,' which also prevails in much contemporary ecumenical theology."[8] Because a "catholic spirit" implied only a bare minimum of doctrine to be believed, it did not interfere with Methodism's "theological pluralism." The "catholic spirit" was used both to identify a common heritage with other Christians and to warrant theological experimentation that expanded, challenged, and critiqued that common heritage.

As noted in Watson's previous chapter, this second interpretation of a "catholic spirit" dominated the 1972 General Conference. In fact, the first interpretation alarmed the 1972 General Conference. Fears were voiced that some would seek to "enforce" our "traditional doctrinal statements and standards" while others would "repeal" them.[9] Despite the fact that the United Methodist *Book of Discipline* continued to state that "chargeable offenses" included "dissemination of doctrines contrary to the established standards of doctrine of the Church," the 1972 *Book of Discipline* guaranteed that such enforcement stood contrary to a Wesleyan "catholic spirit." The two interpretations of a catholic spirit existed side by side in an irresolvable tension from 1972 until 1984.

General Conferences continued to wrestle with what a catholic spirit meant since that initial attempt. The 1984 General Conference, like the 1972, preserved the first interpretation. It stated, "United Methodists never undertake the task of theologizing as a totally new venture. We share a common heritage with all other Christians everywhere and in all ages."[10] General Conference interpreted this "common heritage" primarily in terms of a minimum of doctrine to be believed:

> With them [other Christian churches] we acknowledge belief in the triune God—Father, Son and Holy Spirit. We hold common faith in the mystery of salvation in and through Jesus Christ. We proclaim together that, in our willful alienation God judges us, seeks us, pardons us, and receives us, only because he truly loves us. We therefore believe that the Holy Spirit prompts us to respond in faith and enables us to accept God's gift of reconciliation and justification. This sense of common Christian heritage is rich in our hymnody and liturgies.[11]

---

8. *The Book of Discipline of The United Methodist Church, 1972*, 70.
9. Ibid., 69–70.
10. *The Book of Discipline of The United Methodist Church, 1984*, 73.
11. Ibid., 73–74.

General Conference identifies a "catholic spirit" as belief in the Trinity, salvation in Christ, and the Spirit's work in reconciliation and justification. It notes, but never explores, that the "common heritage" is found in "our hymnody and liturgies." It never asks if that doctrine depends upon the hymnody and liturgy and vice versa. Of course, what the General Conference giveth it can also taketh away.

From 1972 to 1984 General Conference also interpreted the Wesleyan "catholic spirit" in terms of the second interpretation: a "theological pluralism" as an "alternative" to any confessional tradition. The result was an unstable tension, which the 1984 General Conference was tasked to resolve. The 1984 General Conference was charged with addressing "the proper understanding of the catholic spirit, which is often spoken of today as pluralism."[12] It clarified what was meant by a catholic spirit through a more careful articulation of sources and their interrelations for theology. Those clarifications, for all their improvement over the so-called "Wesleyan Quadrilateral" and the theological fragmentation it entailed, nonetheless failed. They did not produce a substantive catholic spirit or address the pressing question how doctrine, worship, and life interact. The 1984 General Conference shared in common with the 1972 General Conference that catholicity is primarily a matter of doctrinal essentials and continued to interpret Wesley's catholic spirit as suggesting a pluralism of worship styles, sacramental practices, and Christian discipleship. Such a fragmentation of doctrine, worship, and life failed to see the close correlations among them. Under these conditions, doctrine is reduced to "belief" as willful assent, and worship and life become a matter of individual preference and style, of "private judgment."

Wesley opened the door to this fragmentation. He stated that a "catholic spirit" did not mean, "'Embrace my modes of worship,' or, 'I will embrace yours.'" Such a statement readily lends itself to the pluralistic, "alternative to any confession" interpretation. But the context for Wesley's argument should not be forgotten. He was speaking to members of the Wesleyan movement who came from different churches. He was not addressing members within a common church, which is obvious in what comes next in his sermon, which seldom gains a hearing. He wrote, "This also is a thing which does not depend either on your choice or mine. We must both act as each is fully persuaded in his own mind."[13] Note the apparent contradic-

12. Heitzenrater, "In Search of Continuity and Consensus," 94.
13. Wesley, "Catholic Spirit," 89.

tion in this sentence. Worship does not depend upon individual choice, but each must be "fully persuaded" as to worship style. If the latter point gets emphasized without attention to the former, then Wesley's statement easily gives the impression that each individual Christian or congregation should choose those modes of worship they find persuasive, but this overlooks the first part of his sentence. Worship does not depend on individual choice. His point is not that each congregation, lay member, or minister should pursue the worship style he or she determines to be authentic. His point is that members of the Wesleyan movement from churches other than the Anglican did not need to follow Anglican worship styles to be part of the movement, and most importantly, the government should not establish a church and require uniformity of worship. Each church represented in the movement had a set worship, and if a member of that church was persuaded by his or her church's worship, then such persons need not use the apparatus of government to impose their mode of worship. They could still seek holiness together. Nonetheless, the mode of worship is not a function of individual choice. Within a church, it is not in the realm of "think and let think."

If Wesley thought a church, grounded in a catholic spirit, could have as diverse worship styles and practices as currently exist in Methodism, he never would have affirmed Article 22, "Of the Rites and Ceremonies of Churches" in the United Methodist "Articles of Religion," an article that continues as a "standard of doctrine" to this day. It provides a better understanding of a catholic spirit than the minimum, "doctrinal essentials" interpretation. That article states:

> It is not necessary that rites and ceremonies should in all places be the same, or exactly alike; for they have been always different, and may be changed according to the diversity of countries, times, and men's manners, so that nothing be ordained against God's Word. Whosoever, through his private judgment, willingly and purposely doth openly break the rites and ceremonies of the church to which he belongs, which are not repugnant to the Word of God, and are ordained and approved by common authority, ought to be rebuked openly, that others may fear to do the like, as one that offendeth against the common order of the church, and woundeth the consciences of weak brethren. Every particular church may ordain, change, or abolish rites and ceremonies, so that all things may be done to edification.[14]

14. *The Book of Discipline of The United Methodist Church, 2012*, 69.

Rites and ceremonies are not subject to "private judgment"; they are a matter of "common authority." Each minister cannot choose for her or himself how to baptize, preside at the Eucharist, or celebrate the liturgical year. To turn such matters into "private judgment" decided by a minister is an egregious form of clericalism that violates communal agreements.

Wesley assumes there are "rites and ceremonies . . . ordained and approved by common authority," but if a church exists that has no such "rites and ceremonies," then all we have is private judgment, which is all Methodism currently has. For that reason, we do not possess any catholic spirit. We have no established rites and ceremonies held in common, providing a measure according to which clerical practice is accountable. Although the *Book of Discipline* once contained "The General Services of the Church," it does so no longer. That shift first took place in 1968 when "orders of worship," "baptism, confirmation and reception," "The Lord's Supper," "marriage" and "burial" were no longer included in the *Book of Discipline*. They were no longer recognized as falling under the common disciplined life of the faithful. Although these services were removed in 1968, Methodism had long since placed them under the realm of "think and let think" since catholicity only required minimal doctrinal essentials. But once worship becomes a matter of private judgment, doctrine loses its intelligibility.

Despite the advantages of the 1984 General Conference's revisions, no common life in doctrine, practice, or worship emerged; it presented no "whole" according to which the ordained or the laity could indicate catholicity. The Wesleyan "catholic spirit" allows each clergy member to decide for him or herself what will be taught, how the liturgy will be performed, and how Methodism relates to the broad consensus that would be a genuine catholic spirit. Because we only have "private judgment" outside a minimal doctrinal essence, there is no way to obey or violate Article 22. Moreover, the adjudicating agencies of the church entrusted with interpreting Methodism's official teaching consistently apply the "alternative to confession" understanding of a catholic spirit regardless of what General Conference or our standards state. Because a catholic spirit requires no more than a minimum of right belief, it legitimates the broadest possible interpretation of that minimum to insure that nothing more than this minimal, excessively Protestant version of a "catholic spirit" will be asked of Methodists. It follows that even a bare minimum of catholicity will be viewed as a threat to the Protestant version of a "catholic spirit." Such a use of catholicity results in doctrinal, liturgical, and practical fragmentation. If the minimum, essential doctrine necessary for belief defines a "catholic spirit," then other central means by which Christianity get mediated—the lives of the saints, sacraments, liturgy, feast days, ethics, general rules—are outside the "essentials" and placed in the realm of "think and let think." Yet doctrine draws on and serves these other essentials. Remove them, and doctrine itself becomes superficial, nothing but a matter of belief. Eventually the realm of "think and let think" defines more and more of the mediation of Christian faith until catholicity is no longer identifiable.

Retrieving a More Robust Catholic Spirit

Clergy and lay trials cannot retrieve a more robust catholic spirit. Doctrine does not exist in the life of the church solely to insure an authoritative regime. Trials, although they may be necessary on occasion, fail to demonstrate why doctrine matters and usually only demonstrate the opposite. Doctrine is, however, essential to Christian practice. Doctrine provides us with means to identify the God we gather to worship and follow. If God cannot be identified at all, God cannot be worshipped. If God cannot be worshipped, creatures cannot participate in the life of God or share in God's wisdom and will. Of course, as Augustine and every other theologian taught, anyone who thinks she or he knows God exhaustively does not know God, which is also an essential Christian doctrine. But the options are not either we know God in full or we have no means of identifying God. That we cannot know God in God's fullness does not entail we cannot know God, and the key term here is "we." Doctrine, like any language, is communal. It is not a private possession one can utilize however one chooses. It is a "common heritage."

Let me conclude with two suggestions on how we might patiently retrieve a more robust catholic spirit and why it is that Wesley's catholic spirit requires this kind of patience and generosity rather than what can only be conceived as a coercive act of power. First, we should situate Wesley's work and his movement otherwise than those interpretations that place him as the founder of a Christian sect or church like Luther or Calvin. Rather than a founder of a Protestant sect that must remain distinctive over and against catholicity, Wesley offers a theological *ressourcement* within catholic Christianity. Second, rather than affirming minimal doctrinal essentials, Wesley's *ressourcement* should be connected to the fullest possible interpretation of catholic Christianity. Here General Rules, creeds, and a common liturgical worship life provide crucial means for retrieving a robust catholicity. Let me explain each suggestion in more detail.

Situating Wesley's work

Wesley's "Catholic Spirit" alone, like his other sermons and works, does not and cannot constitute a robust catholicity. Much more is required. Fortunately, Wesley, unlike Luther or Calvin, was not a significant theologian to whom we must return again and again in order to justify the Wesleyan movement's distinctiveness. To turn him into this kind of theologian and make him the founder of a church does him a disservice, one found in attempts to make Wesley a significant Protestant thinker. Take for instance Albert C. Outler's effort to give Wesley "his place in the history of Protestant thought." Outler argued for this place in his well-known contribution *John Wesley* in the "Christian Library" series. Outler began that work stating: "John Wesley's eminence is secure—as evangelist, reformer, practical genius. Few men in the eighteenth century have left a mark so clear and ineffaceable . . . There is, however, no such consensus in respect of his place in the history of Protestant thought."[15] Outler situated Wesley in a place that required coming up with Wesleyan distinctives. Wesley now had to be different. His work points less to a catholic fullness and more toward his own unique place among Protestant thinkers. To be fair, Outler knew Wesley did not fit such a place well. He rightly referred to Wesley's "doctrinal perspective" as "evangelical catholicism," and he acknowledged that Wesley learned "[f]rom the great scholars of the seventeenth-century revival of patristic studies . . . the intimate correlations of Christian doctrine and Christian spirituality."[16] He stated that Wesley should be known as an "ecumenical theologian" rather than "the eponymous hero of a particular denomination."[17] Nonetheless, he situated Wesley's work in the following way: "It is in some such perspective as this that he is presented here—fully and fairly enough (it is hoped) to demonstrate that [Wesley] shares and contributes to the common concerns of 'A Library of Protestant Thought.'"[18] Wesley must now become something for which he is ill-equipped: a great

---

15. Outler, *John Wesley*, iii.
16. Ibid., v.
17. Ibid., viii.
18. Ibid.

Protestant thinker who, like all *Protestants*, interjects something new and unique—a distinction.

Situating Wesley's work within such a "library" misses something significant. Wesley's work is better situated not in terms of "A Library of Protestant Thought" but in terms of a fullness of evangelical catholicism, which means that Wesley does not so much point to himself but to the riches of the broader catholic tradition. He did so throughout his work, in his *Christian Library*, and elsewhere. Take, for example, his 1756 "Address to the Clergy," in which he asked the clergy if they were competent in metaphysics. Ask yourself, he wrote, "Do I understand metaphysics; if not the depths of the Schoolmen, the subtleties of Scotus or Aquinas, yet the first rudiments, the general principles, of that useful science."[19] That Wesley himself may not have understood Aquinas or Scotus is irrelevant. Wesley was not an original Protestant thinker; he was a witness, pointing to the depths of the catholic tradition for a rich, symphonic *ressourcement* of Christianity.

Methodism should never be a "cult of personality" where we are forced to return to Wesley in search of distinctives. Instead, Wesleyan theology should be a catholic *ressourcement* of evangelical Christianity. The confusing, and perhaps ill-advised, discipline of "Wesley studies" should be less about Wesley alone and more about Wesley and this catholic heritage, following the directions in which he pointed rather than turning him into a significant thinker who accomplished something distinctive. Edgardo Colón-Emeric's *Wesley, Aquinas and Christian Perfection* does this well, acknowledging that Wesley's "house" fits well within Aquinas's "cathedral" and makes good sense there. Anthony Baker's *Diagonal Advance* is another splendid presentation of Wesley's theology that fits his work within a much more catholic conversation, illuminating his strengths and weaknesses. The "Wesleyan Doctrine" series some of us began with Wipf and Stock also seeks to develop this kind of Wesleyan catholic spirit.

Catholic Fullness

Once Wesley's work is situated within a catholic *ressourcement* of evangelical Christianity, it will require us to reconsider "catholicity." It will no longer be defined by minimal doctrinal essentials; these do not define a "catholic spirit." Wesley's sermon is mistitled. It should have been named,

19. Wesley, "An Address to the Clergy," 483.

"Anti-Establishment Christianity." A "catholic spirit" does not characterize a single sermon or idea in Wesley but his corpus, including his reflections on law, sacraments, philosophy, doctrine, and virtues. There is, nonetheless, much to learn from Wesley's mistitled sermon, "Catholic Spirit." Like Wesley we can recognize that Christian churches differ over doctrine and modes of worship, and these differences are not a cause to deny love to brothers and sisters. Like Wesley, we can recognize that these differences in doctrine are not normative but "an unavoidable consequence of the present weakness and shortness of human understanding."[20] We can build on Wesley's recognition that "opinion" and "practice" inevitably go together. But let us also remember what Wesley meant by "think and let think." He stated,

> Although therefore every follower of Christ is obliged by the very nature of the Christian institution to be a member of some particular congregation or other, some church, as it is usually termed (which implies a particular manner of worshipping God; for "two cannot walk together unless they be agreed"); yet none can be obliged by any power on earth but that of his own conscience to prefer this or that congregation to another, this or that particular manner of worship.[21]

The liberty of conscience Wesley affirms in his "Catholic Spirit" rejects the establishment of a church by a "power on earth" based on the nation in which one is born. His liberty of conscience is not a liberty of private judgment on doctrine, worship, and life but a liberty from a state-controlled church, which he identifies as a key principle of the Reformation against "popery."[22] It is a liberty Roman Catholicism has also affirmed since Vatican II.

Wesley's catholic spirit rejects the state imposing doctrine or worship against someone's conscience. It affirms, and requires, that within a church

20. Wesley, "Catholic Spirit," 83.
21. Ibid., 86.
22. Wesley wrote, "I know it is commonly supposed that the place of our birth fixes the church to which we ought to belong; that one, for instance, who is born in England ought to be a member of that which is styled 'the Church of England,' and consequently to worship God in the particular manner which is prescribed by that church. I was once a zealous maintainer of this, but I find many reasons to abate of this zeal. I fear it is attended with such difficulties as no reasonable man can get over. Not the least of which is that if this rule had took place, there could have been no Reformation from popery, seeing it entirely destroys the right of private judgment on which that whole Reformation stands" (ibid.). In the critical apparatus to this sermon, Outler completely misses Wesley's point in this passage, comparing it to Kant's "definition of 'enlightenment'" (ibid., n18).

a common doctrine and worship are present. Within a church, private judgment does not rule; for without a common doctrine and worship, he explicitly states, it is impossible for members of a church "to walk together." If Methodism is to retrieve a catholic spirit, those entrusted with its teaching office will need to reaffirm Wesley's important correlations among doctrine, worship, and life without acting like a state and enforcing them through power.

Wesley's catholicity is found in the General Rules by which the Methodists were to live a common discipline, the creedal Christianity present in the "Articles of Religion," and the common liturgy available in the church's authorized "rites and ceremonies." These are the means of grace which convey the fullness of catholicity. Of course, Wesley consistently warned those who trusted only in the means of grace, the creeds, and the General Rules that they should beware that they do not cultivate a mere "outside religion" at the expense of "heart-religion." Doctrine, rules, and liturgies are means, not ends. That Methodists should not trust in them, however, does not mean they should ignore them or make up their own doctrines, rules, and liturgies based on "private judgment." In fact, Wesley also argued the "religion of the heart" cannot be had without them. For this reason, he warned those that claimed heart religion to beware unless they begin to trust in some internal disposition that refuses any outward demonstration such as keeping the law, confessing the faith, and attending the sacraments. The interplay between the "religion of the heart" and external observance is a consistent theme throughout Wesley's work. He articulated it well in his 1746 preface to *Sermons on Several Occasions*:

> And herein it is more especially my desire, first to guard those who are just setting their faces toward heaven (and who, having little acquaintance with the things of God, are the more liable to be turned out of the way) from formality, from mere outside religion, which has almost driven heart-religion out of the world; and secondly, to warn those who know the religion of the heart, the faith which worketh by love, lest at any time they make void the law through faith, and so fall back into the snare of the devil.[23]

Two warnings are issued. First, Wesley warns those who trust in a mere formality, in outward religion. Second, Wesley warns those who have faith that they not use it to negate the working of the law. The status of creeds and sacraments in Wesley's catholic *ressourcement* is similar to that of the

---

23 Wesley, "Preface" to *Sermons on Several Occasions*, 106.

"law." They are means—externals that in themselves do nothing unless they are also internalized through faith. But if someone thinks faith dispenses with them, such faith is misguided. Far from turning us away from these "externals," it directs us toward them in all their fullness, which is a genuine "catholic spirit."

4

Wesley's Trinitarian Understanding of Holiness

Kenneth M. Loyer

CENTRAL TO JOHN WESLEY'S "practical theology" is the doctrine of salvation, especially this soteriologist's deep-seated concern for holiness in love.[1] While Wesley's thinking on the subject developed over time, one constant feature is that at its essential core his understanding of holiness is an implicitly trinitarian one in which the Holy Spirit figures with particular prominence. The trinitarian foundation is not systematically or exhaustively presented in Wesley's own work, but it remains clearly discernible in his vision of Christian existence. A rediscovery of this foundation can shed light on the theological essence of holiness according to Wesley, which is crucial for correcting perfectionist misreadings that have hindered the reception of this aspect of Wesley's thought virtually from its inception. In these ways, such a rediscovery holds promise for advancing the constructive interpretation of Wesley's doctrine of Christian perfection or, as Wesley often called it, perfect love. Viewing the doctrine through the lens of trinitarian theology clarifies its appropriately theological content and orientation while

---

1. Maddox provides a comprehensive analysis of Wesley's theological works under the heading of "practical theology" in *Responsible Grace*. The above designation of Wesley as a soteriologist represents a way of understanding his life's work that is complementary to the idea of practical theology but also slightly more focused insofar as it highlights the doctrine of salvation, which is a pervasive theme throughout Wesley's sermons and other writings.

illuminating Wesley's emphasis on the immediate and ongoing work of the Holy Spirit sanctifying those in Christ so that the image of God is more fully restored in their lives.

A Theology of Christian Perfection

At the heart of historic Methodist teaching and self-understanding is the doctrine of Christian perfection or entire sanctification, the goal of Christian existence under grace. While the doctrine would find different interpretations throughout Methodist history, the essence of Christian perfection as expressed by Wesley is nothing else than loving God with all of one's heart, soul, and mind and loving one's neighbor as oneself in keeping with the two greatest commandments according to Christ. The doctrine pertains to the gift of God's grace filling the heart, taking up the whole capacity of the soul, and leading believers to perfect obedience to the commands of God. Wesley described Christian perfection as an instantaneous work of God in the soul that is both preceded and followed by a gradual work of grace.[2] Therefore this reality, while beginning at a particular moment in time, is not a static state or isolated momentary event but rather an experience of God's grace that Wesley situates in the broader context of the ongoing journey toward God. Wesley considered the propagation of this doctrine to be one of the chief purposes for which God had raised up Methodism. Indeed, he referred to entire sanctification as the grand *depositum* of Methodism to the world.[3] Although Wesley described the doctrine of Christian perfection as being foundational to the character of a Methodist, he understood it to be not uniquely Methodist in a strict or narrow sense but rather the mark of any genuine Christian.[4] Amidst calls for contemporary Methodists and Wesleyans to reclaim and develop a more compelling theological account of Christian perfection, a possible way forward can be forged through an emphasis on the theme of perfection as participation in God and a renewed appreciation for Wesley's trinitarian understanding of sanctification.

---

2. Wesley, "Brief Thoughts on Christian Perfection," 199.

3. "This doctrine is the grand depositum which God has lodged with the people called Methodists; and for the sake of propagating this chiefly He appeared to have raised us up" ("Letter to Robert Carr Brackenbury, 15 September 1790," 238).

4. See "The Character of a Methodist," 41.

Embodying Wesley's Catholic Spirit

The Need for a More Compelling Theological Account of Christian Perfection

Numerous interpreters of Wesley's writings have recently pointed out the need for a more compelling theological account of Christian perfection. For example, William Abraham makes the quite startling claim that "beyond vague platitudes and rhetorical flourishes [Wesley's] doctrine of Christian perfection is no longer operative" among contemporary Methodists and Wesleyans.[5] If this is indeed the case, the seriousness of the problem can hardly be overstated: "What is at issue is the unraveling of the very core of the tradition . . . Something has gone seriously wrong at the very heart of Methodist doctrine; if the patient is not already dead, it will take strong medicine to effect a cure."[6] What is the "strong medicine" necessary to provide an antidote?

The solution proposed by Abraham emerges from a critical analysis of Wesley's thought that is attentive to the complexities of the doctrine as well as the difficulties intrinsic to Wesley himself. The doctrine is a complex one in part because it consists of what Abraham describes as "an exercise in ascetic theology, a vision of realized eschatology, and a psychology of spiritual development."[7] Wesley's vision of Christian perfection is predicated on the idea that the goal of Christian existence—namely, to be made perfect in love—is actually attainable in this life by God's grace and involves the believer's coming to terms with the problem of guilt and separation from God, the atoning death of Christ, the nature of living faith, repentance and the whole orientation of one's life to God, the assurance of forgiveness of sins, and experienced holiness in the new birth and continued growth in grace for daily life in Christ.[8] The complexity of the life of sanctification according to Wesley is further reflected in the far-reaching set of resources that he made available to those on the journey to holiness. Such resources included not only numerous sermons, tracts, and other writings in which Wesley explicated pertinent conceptual and theological issues from different angles but also his brother's hymns for the learning and singing of the faith, accounts of Christian experiences of sanctification that Wesley published in the *Arminian Magazine*, and recorded minutes in discussions over

---

5. Abraham, "Christian Perfection," 587.
6. Ibid.
7. Ibid.
8. See generally ibid., 590.

doctrinal nuances while in conference with Methodist preachers. Wesley also developed and oversaw an extensive system of societies, classes, and bands for spiritual direction and the promotion of communally accountable Christian discipleship as part of the quest for perfection in love.[9]

Nevertheless, whatever the merits of this complex view of perfection, there are inherent difficulties in Wesley's own account that complicate an attempt to appropriate it. Among the challenges is overcoming the tendency toward anthropocentrism to which Wesley, with his insistence on holiness as the heart of Christianity, opens the door. While the sanctification of human beings in Christ is indeed intrinsic to the message of the gospel, any claim about the centrality of sanctification in Christian teaching and practice must be made carefully lest a theocentric vision be supplanted by an anthropocentric one. Yet that is precisely what happens in Wesley's own sermons, as Abraham asserts, with the generations following Wesley taking an even further anthropocentric turn.[10] The deeper issue here is the problem of reducing the faith to a doctrine of the Christian life. To be sure, faith encompasses the Christian life—the act or experience of faith—but faith properly speaking is about more than simply Christian experience; it is first and foremost about God. The Christian life is a vital manifestation of the faith but is neither its primary subject nor its source. There is both the faith by which one believes (the act of faith) and the faith that is believed (its objective content). The content of the faith pertains to and should inform the lived experience of faith, but without being reduced to that experience. Such a reduction concentrates on the act of faith but does not sufficiently account for the content of the faith as rooted in God's life and revelation. Whether Wesley ultimately succumbs to this problem or not, he clearly heads in that direction at the very least, as in his subtle shift to describe the *analogia fidei*, which traditionally centers on the doctrine of God, in terms

---

9. "Once we locate entire sanctification in the full panoply of biblical exegesis, theological articulation, experiential testimony, and inventive spiritual and ecclesial practices, we can begin to see the massive experiment in the spiritual life that was at the core of Methodism" (ibid., 591).

10. See generally ibid., 593–94. Elsewhere, I offer a survey of contemporary Methodist theology that shows the necessity of grounding sanctification in the doctrine of the Trinity and chiefly in a robust theology of the Holy Spirit; see *God's Love through the Spirit*. In particular, I diagnose the problem of the anthropocentric tendencies in contemporary Methodist theology in chap. 1, which advances the argument that apart from an extensive retrieval effort supported by external assistance, the tradition of John Wesley is imperiled.

of his own more narrowly focused understanding of the way of salvation.[11] In short, Wesley's characteristic concentration on soteriology requires a deeper and broader theological vision than the one that Wesley explicitly articulated himself. Nowhere is this general principle more apposite than in regard to the interpretation of his doctrine of Christian perfection.

When it comes specifically to this doctrine, Abraham argues that the most promising way forward is through the work of grafting the doctrine more deeply into the faith of the church. As he explains, "indeed the history of Methodism shows that the doctrine of perfection cannot survive if its anthropocentric tendencies are not healed by radical immersion in the great sweep of Christian thinking embodied in creation, freedom, fall, and redemption."[12] The task at hand, then, is to enrich Wesley's discoveries and insights through a more robust theological account of perfection that draws from the riches of the Christian tradition and the faith of the church across time and space.[13]

Another scholar calling for a more theological understanding of sanctification in the retrieval and updating of Wesley is Theodore Runyon. In *The New Creation: John Wesley's Theology Today*, Runyon documents the problems of perfectionism (understood as a state of completed perfection) and spiritual elitism that have hindered the full reception of Wesley's doctrine virtually from the outset.[14] In response to these difficulties, Runyon suggests a reinterpretation of the doctrine of Christian perfection with additional emphasis on the perfection of God's love. According to Runyon, God's perfect love is "the most viable starting point" for such a project for two reasons: first, to begin with the perfection of God's love obviates the "preoccupation with self and perfect sinlessness" that has limited some prior interpretations and more closely reflects Wesley's careful avoidance of

---

11. Wesley provides the most extensive explanation of what he means by the "analogy of faith" in his notes on Rom 12:6 in reference to the phrase "Let us prophesy according to the analogy of faith": "St. Peter expresses it, 'as the oracles of God' [1 Pet 4:1]; according to the general tenor of them; according to that grand scheme of doctrine which is delivered therein, touching original sin, justification by faith, and present, inward salvation. There is a wonderful analogy between all these; and a close and intimate connexion between the chief heads of that faith 'which was once delivered to the saints' [Jude 3]. Every article, therefore, concerning which there is any question should be determined by this rule; every doubtful scripture interpreted according to the grand truths which run through the whole" (*Explanatory Notes upon the New Testament*, 569–70).

12. Abraham, "Christian Perfection," 599.

13. See generally ibid., 597–98.

14. See broadly Runyon, *The New Creation*, 91–101 and 222–23.

the phrase "sinless perfection"; second, it "opens" believers to "participation in the only source of genuine sanctification," namely, the grace and love of the triune God.[15] For these reasons, Runyon concludes that to advance the interpretation of Wesley on perfection, Wesley's teaching can profitably be set against the theological backdrop of God's perfect love. Though this love is inexhaustible, God has made it truly accessible to human beings in the opening up of his divine life in Jesus Christ and the invitation for all people to participate in it through the sanctifying grace of the Holy Spirit.

Perfection as Participation in God:
The Love that Sanctifies and the Sanctification of Love

Considering perfection in terms of participation in God's perfect love, as Runyon particularly emphasizes based on his reading of Wesley,

15. Ibid., 231–32. Wesley forcefully rejects claims to "sinless perfection" in "On Sin in Believers," where he allows that believers are delivered from the guilt and power of sin but not the being of it (328). He provides a more detailed discussion in *A Plain Account of Christian Perfection*, in which he quotes an earlier tract entitled "Thoughts on Perfection": "To explain myself a little farther on this head—(1) Not only sin, properly so called (that is, a voluntary transgression of a known law), but sin, improperly so called (that is, an involuntary transgression of a Divine law, known or unknown), needs atoning blood. (2) I believe there is no such perfection in this life as excludes these involuntary transgressions which I apprehend to be naturally consequent on the ignorance and mistakes inseparable from mortality. (3) Therefore, *sinless perfection* is a phrase I never use, lest I should seem to contradict myself. (4) I believe, a person filled with the love of God is still liable to these involuntary transgressions. (5) Such transgressions you may call sins, if you please: I do not, for the reasons above mentioned" (54). Similarly in a 1763 letter, Wesley writes: "What, then, does their arguing prove who object against *perfection*? 'Absolute and infallible *perfection*?' I never contended for it. *Sinless perfection*? Neither do I contend *for this*, seeing the term is not scriptural. A perfection that perfectly fulfils the whole law, and so needs not the merits of Christ? I acknowledge none such—I do now, and always did, protest against it. 'But is there not *sin* in those that are *perfect*?' I believe not; but, be that as it may, they feel none, no temper but pure love, while they rejoice, pray, and give thanks continually. And whether sin is *suspended* or *extinguished*, I will not dispute; it is enough that they feel nothing but love. This you allow 'we should daily press after'; and this is all I contend for. O may God give you to taste of it to-day!" ("Letter to Mrs. Maitland, 12 May 1763," 213). Despite Wesley's care in avoiding the phrase himself, many of his followers understood his doctrine as implying "sinless perfection"; see Peters, *Christian Perfection and American Methodism*. Still, in the face of criticism that any notion of perfection, no matter how qualified, is misleading if not fundamentally erroneous, Wesley justified his use of the word "perfection" itself in, among other places, the aforementioned letter: "As to *the word*, it is scriptural; therefore neither you nor I can in conscience object against it, unless we would send the Holy Ghost to school and teach Him to speak who made the tongue" ("Letter to Mrs. Maitland, 12 May 1763," 212).

underscores the crucial theological point that the love that sanctifies is God's love. God's love is sanctifying insofar as it is this love, and this love only, that makes people holy. Through their participation in God's life by grace, Christians are renewed in the image of God and become holy as God is holy (see Matt 5:48). Wesley consistently propagated such an understanding of what might be called participatory sanctification, as explained more fully below. For now, it is enough simply to note that sanctifying love denotes, first of all, the love that sanctifies the faithful toward the goal of perfection or entire sanctification.

A second meaning of the phrase has to do with the sanctification of the very concept of love. In this sense, the idea of sanctifying love pertains to the identification and safeguarding of an appropriately theological understanding of love that is rooted in and shaped by the Trinity's economy of salvation. Simply put, if it is to be in keeping with Wesley (and, for that matter, with the historic Christian faith), then the way in which people understand love must itself be sanctified in order to ensure its properly theological focus and orientation. Otherwise the conception of love in question would become detached from true holiness and, as such, vulnerable to the kind of sentimentality, self-determination, and likely self-indulgence against which Kenneth Collins rightly cautions.[16] To speak of sanctifying love, however, is to illumine love in a distinct way, setting it apart from other uses, and to clarify that what is under consideration here is not a sentimentalized or self-determined notion of love but precisely the transforming love of God revealed in Jesus Christ and applied to human hearts through the Holy Spirit. This indeed is the love that so captivated the thought of Wesley and animated his vision of the Christian life.

Participation in God is a useful motif for interpreting Wesley on perfection not simply because Wesley employs it in his own writings but also because it points to God as the boundless source of all perfection and sanctifies the very concept of love. Thus, this twofold meaning of the phrase "sanctifying love" resolves a major problem associated with the interpretation of Wesley's doctrine of Christian perfection—namely, perfectionism—while also securing a conception of love that is sanctified by virtue of its basis in the doctrine of God.

Regarding the former, perfectionism denotes the idea that once perfection is attained there is no room for additional growth; in this view the goal has been reached, and the finish line crossed. Yet Wesley taught that

---

16. See generally Collins, *The Theology of John Wesley*, 8–9.

while Christian perfection is the work of God wrought in the faithful soul at a particular moment in time, it is not a static, completed state (perfect*ed* perfection) but an ongoing journey (perfect*ing* perfection), and that with continued growth in grace through faith perfection can always be experienced in higher levels of love.[17] In his commentary on Philippians 3:12, for example, Wesley points out a crucial distinction between being perfect and being perfected: "There is a difference between one that is perfect and one that is *perfected*. The one is fitted for the race (verse 15); the other, ready to receive the prize."[18] Wesley takes St. Paul's references to perfection here to mean being strong and mature in faith, and fit for the race that is not yet completed—hence the directive to press on toward the goal for the prize awaiting us at the end of our journey to God (Phil 3:12, 14). So in contrast to perfectionism, Wesley promoted a view of perfection that was dynamic and always remained open to the possibility of greater growth in love through the continuous activity of the Holy Spirit leading disciples of Jesus Christ toward the goal that is God himself. Wesley could readily affirm such an understanding of participatory sanctification because he taught that along the way of salvation the opportunities for growth are as limitless as the God who is the source, author, and perfecter of salvation. The participation in God's love that is possible here and now can always be deepened—even for those who have been made perfect in love, as God will then further expand their capacity to love. For Wesley, rather than being a static state, perfection is a never-ending aspiration to share in all of love's perfecting fullness.[19] Against any mistaken notion of perfectionism, the first meaning of the phrase "sanctifying love" denotes the Spirit's ongoing work of sanctifying those who are in Christ, of perfecting them in love as they continue, by grace, toward full and final union with God in glory.

Meanwhile, the secondary connotation of sanctifying love is important for the sake of clarification because it calls attention to the theological content and context of love as found in the doctrine of God. What gives Wesley's notion of love its specific meaning, setting it apart from other

---

17. Outler's "Introduction" to "Christian Perfection," 98.

18. Wesley, *Explanatory Notes upon the New Testament*, 735.

19. See Outler's introduction to "Christian Perfection," 98. Langford expounds the idea of "perfection becoming more perfect" by referring to friendship: "The best illustration I can think of is a friendship which is complete and fully good (if there is such a friendship) which by its quality creates new possibility for more completeness" ("John Wesley's Doctrine of Sanctification," 69). This illustration expresses the deeply relational and dynamic features of Wesley's understanding of perfect love.

conceptions of love, is its grounding in the nature and activity of the triune God and especially in the missions of the Son and the Spirit by which the faithful come to share in the life of God. The participatory component in Wesley's doctrine of perfect love—a fuller account of which will follow—ensures that the kind of love in question is precisely the love of God, a love richly shown in Christ and imparted to human lives in all its sanctifying graces through the Spirit.

Consequently, in response to recent calls from Methodist and Wesleyan theologians to rethink sanctification in more compelling theological terms, the study of Wesley can be advanced through a reappraisal of Wesley on sanctification, the interpretive problems that his approach poses, and its potential enhancement via a deeper and clearer grounding in the doctrine of God and the doctrine of the Holy Spirit in particular. Toward that end, a fresh consideration of Wesley's trinitarian understanding of sanctification is in order.

Wesley's Implicitly Trinitarian Doctrine of Christian Perfection

Although the essence of Wesley's approach to sanctification found articulation long before his time in Scripture and ancient Christian writings,[20] Wesley showed a measure of originality in the way he combined various strands of thought, along with several emphases of his own, to account for what he considered the overarching goal of the Christian life, namely, perfection in love of God and neighbor. Wesley's views on perfect love have received no shortage of attention over the years.[21] Here, however, the aim is not to conduct a wholesale examination of this doctrine but rather to analyze and interpret it in light of the doctrine of God in order to explore the bearing of Wesley's understanding of God on his conception of perfection in love. An account of these two subjects will point to a crucial connection between them—a connection that seems intrinsic to Wesley's thought even if he does not provide a systematic or comprehensive explanation of it. That

20. On the scriptural and patristic influences on Wesley's view of Christian perfection (and on his theology as a whole), see Campbell, *John Wesley and Christian Antiquity*.

21. The classic study remains Lindström, *Wesley and Sanctification*. Other noteworthy accounts include Schlimm, "The Puzzle of Perfection"; Hulley, "An Interpretation of John Wesley's Doctrine of Perfect Love"; Arnett, "The Role of the Holy Spirit in Entire Sanctification in the Writings of John Wesley"; and Moore, "Development in Wesley's Thought on Sanctification and Perfection."

connection might be described in this way: Wesley's doctrine of Christian perfection is rooted in the God of perfect love and directed toward human communion with this God, which is to say that the doctrine has an implicitly trinitarian basis and end.

The doctrine of Christian perfection is, at its very core, about love. Yet the subject of this doctrine is not some vague or abstract notion of love. Rather, Wesley's understanding of love has a particular theological focus and finds tangible expression in the life of faith. It deals specifically with the twofold love of which Christ himself speaks, love of God and neighbor (Matt 22:36–40, Mark 12:28–31, Luke 10:25–28). According to Wesley, Christian perfection is perfection in love, though not as in a static state of perfected spiritual completion—the primary misinterpretation that has hindered the reception of this doctrine, as pointed out earlier—but, instead, as denoting the perfect Christian obedience to the commands of God that is made possible by the gift of God's love continually filling the heart. As a result of the ongoing work of the Holy Spirit, the human capacity for love is enlarged; hence, growth in grace toward a more perfect knowledge and love of God is an ever-present possibility. Perfect love involves, in other words, an active, dynamic holiness of heart and life that is embodied in the grace-enabled, wholehearted fulfillment of the two greatest commandments, to love God with one's entire being and to love one's neighbor as oneself, and that can always be experienced in higher levels through the sanctifying grace of the Spirit.[22]

This love-based description is one of three ways in which Wesley summarizes the doctrine in *A Plain Account of Christian Perfection*, a synopsis of his views from 1725 until the time of its composition in 1765. The other two explanations that he provides express the same basic idea of full submission in love to God. In another view, Christian perfection is "purity of intention, dedicating all the life to God."[23] It is a matter of devoting "not a part, but all, our soul, body, and substance" to God.[24] Wesley also describes the doctrine in terms of renewal in the image of God. From this perspective, Christian perfection is a renewal of the heart in "the full likeness of

---

22. In his sermon of the same title, Wesley says that Christian perfection is "only another term for holiness." And as he goes on to clarify, there is always room for growth in grace toward a more perfect knowledge and love of God, hence the dynamic quality of Christian perfection in his understanding (see "Christian Perfection," 104–5).

23. *A Plain Account of Christian Perfection*, 117.

24. Ibid.

Him that created it."²⁵ It entails having the mind that was in Christ and thereby walking as Christ walked. While each of these summaries has its own nuances, Wesley maintains that there is no material difference among the three. In fact, all three point to the proper backdrop against which perfection becomes intelligible—the doctrine of God.

Although Wesley's decidedly practical focus did not compel him to outline in systematic fashion the relationship between trinitarian theology and his conception of holiness, he seems to have assumed this backdrop.²⁶ Christian perfection or perfection in love has a trinitarian basis and end, each of which is intrinsic to Wesley's thought. Even if this trinitarian content is not exhaustively developed in his own writings, it can be unearthed and put to a constructive purpose.

That the doctrine of Christian perfection has an implicit trinitarian basis and end is indicated by two crucial themes in Wesley. The first is God's action in salvation history, which establishes the basis of the doctrine, and the second is the human communion with God made possible by this action, a communion that constitutes the doctrine's end, or more precisely our end as described in the doctrine. In order to explore the connection between Wesley's understanding of God and his conception of perfection in love, each of these themes will now be scrutinized in turn.

---

25. Ibid.

26. That Wesley seems to have assumed a trinitarian grounding for his conception of holiness is an example of what Deschner describes as Wesley's "presupposed theology." In his study of Wesley's Christology, Deschner observes that Wesley expressed his theology "on several levels." Deschner classifies these levels in a threefold manner: "the articulated theology of [Wesley's] writings, the presupposed theology behind the writings, and the enacted theology of his praxis." As Deschner goes on to explain, Wesley's "presupposed theology is for the most part the source-theology which underlies the Sermons: especially the ecumenical traditions of the Articles, but also to some degree the patristic, Anglican, puritan, pietist, and mystical influences which shaped his mind. It is important to recognize that this presupposed theology is not Wesley's unconscious theology, or some speculation on our part about what he might have thought, but a quite intentional level of Wesley's considered and settled theological understanding: the level of his Trinitarianism, of his christology, of his ecclesiology—themes which were absolutely fundamental in his theology, but which he did not emphasize when he preached at street corners" (*Wesley's Christology*, xii).

God's Saving Action: The Trinitarian Basis of Christian Perfection

The doctrine of Christian perfection or perfection in love is firmly founded upon the economy of God's salvation and thus is grounded in God's saving actions in and for the world. Wesley provides one of the clearest and most comprehensive accounts of his vision of salvation in the sermon "The Scripture Way of Salvation." In specifically trinitarian fashion he explicates his understanding of salvation, which encompasses:

> all the "drawings" of "the Father" [John 6:44], the desires after God, which, if we yield to them, increase more and more; all that "light" wherewith the Son of God "enlighteneth everyone that cometh into the world" [John 1:9], *showing* every man "to do justly, to love mercy, and to walk humbly with his God" [Micah 6:8]; all the *convictions* which his Spirit from time to time works in every child of man.[27]

For Wesley, salvation is "the differentiated but united work of the Three Persons of the Godhead."[28] This work sets us into proper relationship to each of the three persons and (to anticipate the next heading) effects our participation in their divine communion. Through the drawings of the Father, the illumination of the Son, and the convictions of the Holy Spirit, we come by grace to experience God's salvation. As Wesley goes on to explain, the salvation of which Paul speaks in the focal verse of this sermon (Eph 2:8) is a matter of both justification and sanctification. Justification, or pardon through the blood and righteousness of Christ, denotes (as Wesley elsewhere describes) "what God *does for us* through his Son," while sanctification, the inward renewal produced by the Holy Spirit, signifies "what [God] *works in us* by his Spirit."[29] Justification restores us "to the favour, [and sanctification] to the image of God."[30] In a slight elaboration, Wesley explains in another sermon that such a renewal in the divine image involves holiness and deliverance from bondage to sin: "By justification we are saved from the guilt of sin, and restored to the favour of God: by sanctification we are saved from the power and root of sin, and restored to the image of

---

27. "The Scripture Way of Salvation," 156–57.
28. Wainwright, *Methodists in Dialog*, 269.
29. Wesley, "Justification by Faith," 187. See also his "The Scripture Way of Salvation," 157–58.
30. Wesley, "The Great Privilege of Those That Are Born of God," 432.

God."[31] In regard to both justification and sanctification, the action of God is central and, indeed, pervasive. It is in such action on our behalf, as well as within our very hearts and minds, that human salvation chiefly consists.

Having thus laid the foundation of his soteriology, Wesley builds upon this foundation at the end of the first section of "The Scripture Way of Salvation." There he refers to entire sanctification or the "full salvation" for which Christ's followers wait.[32] Closely related to these terms is the Pauline directive to go on to perfection (see Phil 3:12), that is, to perfect love—the love that excludes sin, fills the heart, and takes up "the whole capacity of the soul."[33] Christian perfection for Wesley is the consummation of salvation, the culmination of God's saving work in and for us. As such it is the goal toward which all the faithful are called to strive.

In "The Scripture Way of Salvation," Wesley identifies faith as the one condition for salvation. Wesley's conception of faith is linked to his notion of the spiritual senses through which human beings come to know God. Faith implies, Wesley says, "both a supernatural *evidence* of God and of the things of God, a kind of spiritual *light* exhibited to the soul, and a supernatural *sight* or perception thereof."[34] Through the operation of the Holy Spirit, opening and enlightening the eyes of the soul, Christians are able to see things that the natural eye cannot see. The illuminating work of God opens up a whole new world, "the *spiritual world*, which is all round about us, and yet no more discerned by our natural faculties than if it had no being."[35] In an even more particular sense, Wesley describes faith as a divine evidence and conviction of the saving grace of Christ not only for the world as a whole but also for the individual believer.[36] Their spiritual senses having been stimulated, those in Christ come by faith to know God themselves—to see, touch, hear, and taste the salvation made possible by the gracious action of the triune God. That is, they are thus able, first of all, to discern that in Holy Scripture God has promised salvation to its fullest, to perfection in love; second, to trust that what God has promised he is able

---

31. Wesley, "On Working Out Our Own Salvation," 204.
32. See Wesley, "The Scripture Way of Salvation," 160.
33. Ibid.
34. Ibid.
35. Ibid., 161.
36. See ibid.

to perform; and third, to believe that perfection in love is possible, through God's grace, even now.[37]

Wesley's discussion of Christian perfection is predicated upon the understanding of salvation that he sets forth in "The Scripture Way of Salvation," and that understanding is itself shaped by God's saving acts in and for the world. Christian perfection therefore assumes, and indeed relies upon, the prior and enabling work of the triune God in salvation history. It is only because of the Father's sending of the Son and the gift of their common Spirit to the church at Pentecost that such a notion as Christian perfection is even conceivable. It is, in other words, only through the very manifestation of God's love to the world in Christ and the outpouring of his love into the hearts of the faithful through the Holy Spirit, that it is possible for human beings to come to the saving knowledge of God and so to share in the life of divine love.[38] The doctrine of Christian perfection has its sole foundation in the triune God's decisive action in the economy of salvation.[39]

Wesley gives concise expression to the trinitarian basis of love in one of one his final sermons, "The Unity of the Divine Being." There he writes, "It is in consequence of our knowing God loves us that we love him, and love our neighbour as ourselves."[40] Wesley grounds the idea of love of God and neighbor, which is one of the most recurring themes in his writings, in God's prior and enabling love for the human family. In the Christian life, our love for God is rooted in God's love for us, as that love is revealed through God's gracious actions in salvation history. The same is true for our love of neighbor, which also follows from the knowledge of God's love for us. As Wesley sees it, the love of God is so strong and dynamic that the true knowledge of it—a knowledge gained through one's experience

---

37. See ibid., 167–68.

38. In "Christian Perfection," Wesley asserts that the miracle-working power of the Holy Spirit was given when Jesus first sent the apostles to preach the gospel (see Matt 10:1 and 8), but that "the Holy Ghost was not yet given in his sanctifying graces, as he was after Jesus was glorified." It was on the day of Pentecost that those who "waited for the promise of the Father" (see Acts 1:4) were made "more than conquerors over sin by the Holy Ghost given unto them"; so "this great salvation from sin was not given till Jesus was glorified" (110–11).

39. Perceiving the significance of the economy of salvation in Wesley's theological teaching and preaching, Vickers claims that "in the light of his doctrines of the atonement and the work of the Holy Spirit, Wesley is rightly viewed as a theologian of the economic Trinity" (*Wesley*, 84).

40. Wesley, "The Unity of the Divine Being," 67.

of God[41]—produces in faithful hearts genuine love for God and for their neighbors. Wesley's conception of love for God and neighbor, and therefore his understanding of perfection in love, is based specifically in the triune God. The foundation of Christian perfection is the very God who has opened his life to us in Christ and renews his own loving image in human hearts by the indwelling Spirit such that we are to become "Transcripts of the Trinity."[42] That last point, suggestive of the communion with God that is made possible by grace, introduces the next stage of this inquiry, the end of Christian perfection.

Communion with God: The Trinitarian End of Christian Perfection

The end of Christian perfection is a matter of communion with God, personal union with the three-person God. As Wesley writes in his sermon "Spiritual Worship" on 1 John 5:20, the Epistle's writer treats directly "the foundation of all, the happy and holy communion which the faithful have with God the Father, Son, and Holy Ghost."[43] This communion is, for Wesley, the orienting vision of life. Alluding to the Augustinian dictum, he recalls that God has made human beings for himself, and that their hearts cannot rest until they rest in him.[44] Through his saving work, the God who has created us for communion with himself draws us into his own life so that we become partakers of the divine nature (see 2 Pet 1:4).

The connection between happiness and holiness runs deep in this sermon, as it does elsewhere in Wesley's writings.[45] The pursuit of happiness, like the pursuit of holiness, is one that finds fulfillment in God: "In this

---

41. The question of the accuracy and sufficiency of Outler's so-called "Wesleyan Quadrilateral" remains a hotly contested issue among Wesley's interpreters, as noted already in the chapters of this volume. While this is not the place for a detailed engagement with that debate, suffice it to say that to the extent that experience had any theological significance for Wesley, it was (as Kevin Watson notes in his contribution) not experience of the world in general but precisely experience of God—especially the experience of God's grace in regeneration and sanctification—that was of greatest importance.

42. "A Collection of Hymns for the Use of the People Called Methodists," 88.

43. Wesley, "Spiritual Worship," 89–90.

44. See Wesley, "Spiritual Worship," 97; as well as his "The Unity of the Divine Being," 63–64.

45. For example, see Wesley's "God's Love to Fallen Man," 425–31; and "The Righteousness of Faith," 209. See also Miles, "Happiness, Holiness, and the Moral Life."

alone can you find the happiness you seek—in the union of your spirit with the Father of spirits; in the knowledge and love of him who is the fountain of happiness, sufficient for all the souls he has made."[46] According to Wesley, this union, knowledge, and love consist in the indwelling of God in the hearts of Christian believers. Happiness, like holiness, begins and ends in God. It begins "when it pleases the Father to reveal his Son in our hearts; when we first know Christ, being enabled to 'call him Lord by the Holy Ghost' [1 Cor 12:3]; when we can testify, our conscience bearing us witness in the Holy Ghost, 'the life which I now live, I live by faith in the Son of God, who loved me, and gave himself for me' [Gal 2:20]."[47] It is then "that heaven is opened in the soul, that the proper, heavenly state commences, while the love of God, as loving us, is shed abroad in the heart [Rom 5:5], instantly producing love to all mankind."[48] The God who freely pours his love into faithful hearts through the Holy Spirit is also the end of happiness, the one toward whom Wesley's account of the Christian life is irrevocably directed. As those who believe advance in the knowledge and love of God, they reach maturity in Christ, to the point of being filled with him, of being completely happy through God's indwelling in them and their continual rest in him:

> when "Christ in us, the hope of glory" [Col 1:27], is our God and our all; when he has taken the full possession of our heart; when he reigns therein, without a rival, the Lord of every motion there; when we dwell in Christ, and Christ in us, we are one with Christ, and Christ with us; then we are completely happy; then we live all "the life that is hid with Christ in God" [Col 3:3]. Then, and not till then, we properly experience what that word meaneth, "God is love; and whosoever dwelleth in love, dwelleth in God, and God in him" [1 John 4:16].[49]

The happiness for which God has made all human beings becomes a reality through the mutual indwelling between God and the faithful. By means of this personal communion, those who are in Christ learn the meaning of the biblical teaching that "God is love" (1 John 4:16). Indeed, they learn God's love and come to abide in it even as they abide in God. For Wesley this is the way to true happiness and holiness; the path to perfection is one

46. Wesley, "Spiritual Worship," 101.
47. Ibid., 96.
48. Ibid.
49. Ibid., 96–97.

of participation in God—a life of constant communion with the Father, the Son, and the Holy Spirit.

The idea of constant communion has eucharistic overtones, which illustrate the reality of participation in God in this life and its link to perfection in love. In his sermon entitled "The Duty of Constant Communion," Wesley stresses the importance of Christians receiving the sacrament not just frequently but, as it were, constantly—that is, as often as God provides them the opportunity. There are spiritually significant benefits to receiving the Eucharist, namely, "the forgiveness of our past sins and the present strengthening and refreshing of our souls."[50] God's grace conveyed in this sacrament confirms to Christians the pardon of their sins because, as Wesley asks rhetorically, "what surer way have we of procuring pardon from [God] than the 'showing forth the Lord's death' [1 Cor 11:26], and beseeching him, for the sake of his Son's sufferings, to blot out all our sins?"[51] The Lord's Supper also nourishes the soul; it is "the food of our souls," which "gives strength to perform our duty, and leads us on to perfection."[52] A gift of God's mercy, this sacrament is a means for the baptized[53] to "obtain holiness on earth and everlasting glory in heaven."[54] Through their communion with God in the life of faith and especially in the Eucharist, Christians grow in grace and are strengthened to live in obedience to God as they continue the journey toward perfection in love that is ultimately perfection in God.[55]

While continued growth in communion with God is possible for believers at present, as John Wesley in particular tirelessly asserts throughout his writings on perfection, he also maintains that its full manifestation will come eschatologically. Wesley expresses this hope in trinitarian fashion

---

50. Wesley, "The Duty of Constant Communion," 429.

51. Ibid.

52. Ibid.

53. The currently fashionable idea of "Open Communion" in The United Methodist Church, when taken to the extreme of meaning not simply ecumenical openness but the communing of non-baptized persons as a purportedly evangelistic measure, represents a departure from both Wesley and the broader Christian tradition. Wesley could assume baptism as it was nearly universal among English citizens of his day. Wesley's reference to the sacrament as a "*converting* ordinance" denotes conversion from one degree of faith to another, higher degree (Journal Entry, "27 June 1740," 158). Also note the following, "there are *degrees in faith*, and *weak faith* may yet be *true faith*" (Journal Entry, "22 June 1740," 155).

54. Wesley, "The Duty of Constant Communion," 432.

55. The sanctifying benefits of the sacrament find poetic articulation in a collection of hymns published jointly by John and Charles Wesley, HLS.

at the close of his sermon "The New Creation": "And to crown all, there will be a deep, an intimate, an uninterrupted union with God; a constant communion with the Father and his Son Jesus Christ, through the Spirit; a continual enjoyment of the Three-One God, and of all the creatures in him!"[56] When it is viewed in eschatological perspective, the trinitarian end of Christian perfection comes clearly into focus. Wesley's emphasis on continued growth in grace gives his conception of perfection a dynamic quality, ensuring that his teaching on perfection includes the present but always points beyond it to even higher levels of holy love that can be experienced by God's grace. Ultimately, it points toward the consummation of God's saving purposes in the sealing of the union between Creator and creature in glory. While this doctrine calls Christians at present to press on in grace toward ever-deepening embodiment of love for God and neighbor, it is also an anticipation of that perfect communion with God that all who dwell in God will forever enjoy.

Therefore, Wesley's doctrine of Christian perfection is related in important ways to the doctrine of the triune God. Implicitly, Wesley's conception of perfect love can be said to have a trinitarian basis by virtue of its firm grounding in God's saving action in and for the world. The end of this doctrine is found to be equally trinitarian, for although the connection between trinitarian theology and perfection is not thoroughly explicated by Wesley, upon analysis of his thought one can justifiably conclude that Wesley's vision of perfection derives its dynamism from the doctrine of God and the reality of Christian participation in God by way of the indwelling and operations of the Holy Spirit. As Christians experience God through their spiritual senses, they come to a deeper knowledge of God and a greater love for God and neighbor, unto the perfection that is attainable by God's grace. In other words, through the work of the Holy Spirit they are renewed in the divine image and drawn increasingly into the triune life of the God whose "darling attribute" is love.[57]

---

56. Wesley, "The New Creation," 510. For a study of Wesley's holistic trinitarian account of the new creation, see Loyer, "'And to Crown All.'"

57. Commenting on 1 John 4:8, Wesley referred to love as God's "darling, His reigning attribute, the attribute that sheds an amiable glory on all His other perfections" (*Explanatory Notes upon the New Testament*, 914).

Conclusion

With his doctrine of Christian perfection, Wesley pinpoints (however latently, given his practical concerns) the end of trinitarian doctrine: entire sanctification for all believers in and by the living God. His thought is animated by a participatory understanding of the doctrines of God and salvation that emphasizes the work of the Holy Spirit. That Wesley's implicitly trinitarian account of sanctification has a vigorous pneumatological component is indicated by his conception of the spiritual senses through which human beings come to experience God, his attention to the soteriological theme of renewal in God's image, and his characteristic emphasis on love and holiness in the Spirit. It is for such reasons as these that Wesley is recognized as one who accentuates the activity and personhood of the Spirit more than many Western thinkers.[58] Although Wesley did not synthesize his insights into a comprehensive system of thought, this pneumatological component provides resources for the development of a theology of holiness and love that is truly "Spiritual," which is to say, related especially closely to the Spirit of holiness and love. The sort of more robust theological account of Christian perfection called for by a number of Wesley's interpreters can indeed be developed with considerable support from Wesley. The spiritual and theological insights and intuitions of Wesley—some distinctively Methodist and others strikingly catholic—can be affirmed and advanced by more clearly connecting sanctification to the Christian doctrine of God. That is one of the great challenges and opportunities facing theologians and practitioners in the Wesleyan-Methodist tradition today.

---

58. See Shults and Hollingsworth, *The Holy Spirit*, 62.

5

Participating in Grace
*Augustine and Wesley
as Preachers of Sanctification*

_____Scott Dermer_____

IN HIS BIOGRAPHY OF the bishop of Hippo, Peter Brown stated that Augustine's thought "marks the end of a long-established classical ideal of perfection."[1] Brown argued that Augustine abandoned his early belief in human perfection and came to insist, especially against the Pelagians, that the human person under grace is subject to a continual battle against sin in this life. Brown wrote that "the alternative offered by Augustine, the heroic endurance of unresolved tensions, might seem to mock all Christian hopes for a new life."[2] Augustine's thought on perfection, in Brown's reading, was a departure not only from the philosophical culture of his time but also from the "great tradition of Western Christianity," which was far more hopeful with regard to the possibilities for human transformation.[3]

Similar to Brown, Wesleyan scholars have noted Augustine's pessimism about the possibilities for human transformation. They have emphasized that such pessimism is at odds with John Wesley's vision of the

---

1. Brown, *Augustine of Hippo*, 150.
2. Ibid., 371.
3. Brown, *Religion and Society in the Age of Saint Augustine*, 200.

Christian life, a vision that centers on the belief that perfection is attainable in this life. For instance, in his historical study of the doctrine of holiness, Paul Basset observed that Augustine's thought diverges from Wesley's because the former holds that entire sanctification is a reality only for the life to come.[4] According to Basset, one finds in Augustine's work a doctrine of holiness "forged in the less hopeful mode."[5]

Wesley himself was not hesitant to refute Augustine on this very point.[6] In his 1784 sermon "The Wisdom of God's Counsels," he lambasts the bishop of Hippo and comes to the defense of Pelagius on the issue of perfection:

> I would not affirm, that the arch-heretic of the fifth century [Pelagius] (as plentifully as he has been bespattered for many ages) was not one of the holiest men of that age, not excepting St. Augustine himself—a wonderful saint! as full of pride, passion, bitterness, censoriousness, and as foul-mouthed to all that contradicted him as George Fox himself. I verily believe the real heresy of Pelagius was neither more nor less than this, the holding that Christians may by the grace of God (not without it; that I take to be a mere slander,) "go on to perfection"; or, in other words, "fulfill the law of Christ."
>
> "But St. Augustine says"—When Augustine's passions were heated his word is not worth a rush. And here is the secret. St. Augustine was angry at Pelagius. Hence he slandered and abused him (as his manner was) without either fear or shame. And St. Augustine was then in the Christian world what Aristotle was afterwards. There needed no other proof of any assertion than *ipse dixit*—"St. Augustine said it."[7]

---

4. See Bassett, *Holiness Teaching*, 164.

5. Bassett and Greathouse, *Exploring Christian Holiness*, 87. Commenting on Augustine, Basset writes: "We seek in vain for any doctrine of sanctification that would indicate completion of the process in this life except insofar as sanctification is completed in essence, but not in fact, at the time of baptism" (105).

6. English ("References to St. Augustine in the Works of John Wesley") notes that Augustine is mentioned forty or more times in the *Works of John Wesley* (1872). English also observes that Augustine is mentioned forty-four times in Wesley's writings in the *Arminian Magazine*. Wesley refers to Augustine more than any other church father, invoking his authority on a broad range of topics: providence, the problem of evil, the church, the sacraments, the authority of scripture, the law, orthodoxy, and salvation. Yet he also challenges Augustine's authority, particularly in regard to grace, predestination, and perfection.

7. Wesley, "The Wisdom of God's Counsels," 555–56.

John English may be right when he observes that Wesley's comments here reflect more his frustrations with his own Calvinist opponents, who frequently cited the bishop of Hippo, than with Augustine himself.[8] What is clear from this passage is that, for Wesley, Augustine is above all a polemicist, whose harsh temperament toward Pelagius led him to a hardened position on the doctrine of perfection.[9]

In considering Augustine's vision of holiness in relation to Wesley's, which is the purpose of this chapter, I propose that we would do well to focus less on Augustine the polemicist and more on Augustine the preacher. Because *like* Wesley, Augustine's principal responsibility was to provide spiritual direction to the souls entrusted to his care, a responsibility that he fulfilled through regular preaching. Augustine's contemporaries viewed his sermons as the most important part of his labors, not his treatises. Possidius, Augustine's first biographer, wrote that in contrast to those who benefitted from reading his treatises, "I believe that they were able to derive greater good from him who heard and saw him as he spoke in person in the church."[10]

In what follows, I will describe the main aspects of Augustine's understanding of sanctification, as it is presented in a selection of sermons on the Gospel of John. These sermons, preached from 406 to 421, offer a nuanced vision of holiness that centers on the believer's participation in Christ.[11] I will then turn to Wesley's understanding of sanctification, as it is presented specifically in his 1781 sermon, "The End of Christ's Coming." This sermon offers a vision of holiness that is rooted in the mission of the Son in human history. By looking at both Augustine and Wesley's sermons, I hope to show not only the variances in their respective visions of holiness, but also their profound and surprising consistencies.

---

8. See English, "References to St. Augustine," 13–14.

9. Wesleyan readers of Augustine have followed suit in viewing the bishop as primarily a polemicist. Bassett (*Exploring Christian Holiness*, 108) states that "most of Augustine's doctrinal development came in the white heat of controversy. The case against the opponent was put in its worst possible light and one's own case was stated with a sharpness and lack of qualification that calmer deliberation would rectify."

10. Latin: "Sed ego arbitror plus ex eo proficere potuisse, qui eum et loquentem in ecclesia praesentem audire et videre potuerunt"; Possidius, *The Life of Saint Augustine*, 58.

11. Augustine's 124 *Tractates on the Gospel of John* were produced in essentially three segments. The dating of Berrouard has gained general acceptance. Berrouard divides the sermons into the following groups with these dates: 1–16 (406/407); 17–19 and 23–54 (414); 55–124 (419); and 20–22 (418–419). See Berrouard, *Introduction aux homélies de Saint Augustin*, 22–27, 79–102, and 177–200.

Participating in Christ: Augustine on Sanctification

In his sermons on John, Augustine presents a deeply Christocentric account of sanctification. In this account, sinful human beings are renewed only through the divine Word who was made flesh. The account is no doubt shaped by John's magnificent prologue. Augustine's three sermons on the prologue naturally focus on the co-eternity and equality of the Word with the Father. His concern in these sermons, however, is soteriological at the core: If the Word is a creature, Augustine reasons against the "Arians," then the Word cannot be the source of human renewal.[12] A creature cannot renew another creature. The preacher warns his congregation: "Do not therefore believe that the Word, through which all things were made, was made, or else you will fail to be made new by the Word, through which all things are made new."[13]

From the outset, then, Augustine establishes that the possibility of human transformation depends on the Word's divine nature. It also depends on the Word's participation in human nature. Augustine holds that the incarnation of the Word is the supreme instance of grace. In the incarnation, the Word assumed human nature not on the basis of its prior merits but by grace.[14] The Word's gratuitous assumption of human nature results in the transformation of that nature. Augustine uses several images to describe this transformation. First, the incarnate Word heals the sick and weakened nature that is inherited from Adam. The Word's flesh is the remedy for human blindness, and his humility is the antidote to human pride, the origin of all sin.[15] Second, the incarnate Word restores the image of God to the human person by destroying the sin of Adam.[16] Third, prompted by John 1:12 ("he gave them the power to become children of God"), Augustine holds that the incarnate Word makes possible the adoption of human beings as

---

12. Recent scholarship has clarified that the term "Arian" is a polemical category in Augustine. It refers not to the theology of Arius and his immediate followers but to the theology of another anti-Nicene group: the Homoians, who held that the Father and the Son are like one another but do not share a common divine nature. See Barnes, "Anti-Arian Works," 31–34.

13. Latin: "Noli ergo credere factum, per quod facta sunt omnia: ne non reficiaris per Verbum, per quod reficiuntur omnia." *In Johannis*, 6–7; *Homilies on the Gospel of John 1–40*, 48.

14. See *In Johannis*, 553.

15. See ibid., 256.

16. See ibid., 107.

children of God. The condition for adoption is forgiveness of sins, which is a free gift received by faith in baptism.[17] This adoption entails nothing other than participation in the divine nature. As he is wont to do, Augustine describes adoption in terms of deification, a concept that scholars traditionally confine to the Greek fathers.[18] Commenting on John 1:12 in a letter to Honoratus, the bishop states that the Son of God "came in order to become the Son of Man and to give to us, who were already human children, the gift of becoming children of God . . . He, therefore, descended in order that we might ascend, and, while remaining in his nature, he became a partaker of our nature in order that we, while remaining in our nature, might become partakers of his nature."[19] By participation in the Son, Augustine holds, human beings become god-like.

The point of departure for Augustine's account of sanctification, then, is the person of the Son and his work in the economy of salvation. The incarnation of the Son has made possible healing from sin, restoration of the deformed image, and transformation of human beings into children of God. For Augustine, the gift of the indwelling Spirit unites human beings to Christ and makes them participants in his divine nature.

Throughout his sermons on John, Augustine emphasizes the depth of the union between believers and Christ. Believers are so deeply united to Christ through the Spirit that they constitute one person with him, the *totus Christus*. Augustine uses strong, realistic language to describe the believer's union with Christ: "Therefore, let us rejoice and give thanks, not only that we have been made Christians, but that we have been made Christ. Do you understand, brothers, do you comprehend the grace of God upon us? Be in awe. Rejoice. We have been made Christ. For he is the head, we are

---

17. See ibid., 17–18.

18. Augustine links together the themes of adoption and deification by associating John 1:12 with Psalm 82:6 in *In Johannis*, 459. For a discussion of these two concepts, see Bonner, "Augustine's Conception of Deification"; Rist, *Augustine*, 259–60; and Meconi, *The One Christ*, chap. 3. Scholars of Wesley typically assume that deification is a Greek patristic notion. See, for example, Outler, "John Wesley's Interests in the Early Fathers of the Church"; and also Maddox, *Responsible Grace*, who argues that Wesley's "understanding of sanctification has significant parallels with the Eastern Orthodox theme of deification (theosis)" (122).

19. Latin: "[filius dei] venit, ut fieret filius hominis donaretque nobis, qui eramus filii hominis, filios dei fieri . . . Descendit ergo ille, ut nos ascenderemus, et manens in sua natura factus est particeps naturae nostrae, ut et nos manentes in natura nostra efficeremur participes naturae ipsius." *Epistulae* 190.162; *Letters 100–155*, 249.

the members—a whole man, he and we."²⁰ The effect of God's grace on the believer is nothing other than real identification with Christ.

As members of the whole Christ, believers share in Christ's own holiness. Augustine expresses this notion with great clarity in his comments on the high priestly prayer in John 17. In John 17:16, Christ states that the disciples do not belong to the world, just as he does not belong to the world. According to Augustine, Christ has never belonged to the world (that is, the world of sin) because he was *born* of the Holy Spirit. The disciples no longer belong to the world because they have been *reborn* of the Holy Spirit. Their regeneration is sanctification. Augustine identifies Christ as the agent of the believer's sanctification. Jesus had said, "And for them do I sanctify myself, so that they also may be sanctified in truth" (John 17:19). According to Augustine, Christ sanctifies himself in the sense that he sanctifies the members of his body. This sanctification refers to an initial transformation in baptism but also to an ongoing transformation as the believer participates in grace. According to the bishop, "even after being sanctified, they [the disciples] advance in the same sanctity and become more saintly, and this, not without the help of God's grace, but because he who sanctified their beginning sanctifies their advancement."²¹

For Augustine, this gradual sanctification in Christ entails genuine deliverance from sin. Augustine connects John 17:19 ("that they also may be sanctified in truth") to John 8:32 ("the truth will make you free") in order to describe this deliverance. In Sermon 41, he reflects at length on the extent to which the truth (that is, Christ himself) liberates human beings from sin in this life. He first points his listeners to God's work in the economy. Christ is able to deliver human beings from the slavery of sin because he came without sin and became the true sacrifice for sin. "This is our hope, brothers, that we be set free by the one who is free."²² For Augustine, Christ brings human beings into real freedom. Yet, the bishop clarifies, there is a clear difference between the freedom that can be had in this life

---

20. Latin: "Ergo gratulemur et agamus gratias, non solum nos christianos factos esse, sed Christum. Intellegitis, fratres, gratiam Dei super nos capitis? Admiramini, gaudete, Christus facti sumus. Si enim caput ille, nos membra; totus homo, ille et nos." *In Johannis*, 216; *Tractates on the Gospel of John 11–27*, 186.

21. Latin: "et sanctificati in eadem proficiunt sanctitate, fiuntque sanctiores; neque hoc sine adiutorio gratiae Dei, sed illo eorum sanctificante provectum, qui sanctificavit incoeptum." *In Johannis*, 616–17; *Tractates on the Gospel of John 55–111*, 280.

22. Latin: "Haec spes nostra est, fratres, ut a libero liberemur." *In Johannis*, 362; *Tractates on the Gospel of John 28–54*, 143.

and the "full and perfect freedom" found in the life to come.[23] In this life, freedom consists in the absence of crimes (*crimen*) or serious sins (*peccatum grave*).[24] Through the grace of baptism a person dies to such sins. However, after baptism there remains a weakness (*infirmitas*) that a faithful person must struggle against until death.[25] Augustine describes this weakness as *concupiscentia*. In the bishop's thought, concupiscence is an abiding inclination or desire for sin (*desiderium peccati*). It is inherited from Adam and it leads to actual sin.[26] In his view, it would be prideful for one to claim to be without *concupiscentia* in this life. John the evangelist himself warned against such pride when he wrote, "If we say that we do not have sin, we deceive ourselves and the truth is not in us" (1 John 1:8). For the bishop, the Christian life will consist of a continual struggle against concupiscence. Augustine often describes the struggle by appealing to Romans 7 and Galatians 5. Augustine holds that Paul, in both passages, is speaking about a person who is *sub gratia*. The person *sub gratia* sees another law in his members which is opposed to the law of his spirit (Rom 7:23). The person *sub gratia* is engaged in an ongoing battle in which flesh lusts against spirit and spirit against flesh (Gal 5:17).[27] For Augustine, the freedom from sin made possible by Christ in this life is real but partial. The Christian life, on this side of the *eschaton*, will always be marked by struggle. To deny the reality of this struggle and affirm the reality of perfection is an act of pride.

Yet it is striking the extent to which Augustine exhorts his congregation to make *progress* in the battle against the desire for sin. By refusing to consent to this desire, the Christian can diminish its power over time. Augustine holds out to his congregation the hopeful possibility of attaining higher levels of freedom from sin in this life. He urges his flock to restrain sins like anger and lust: "Does anger arise? Give not the tongue to anger for uttering abuse . . . This irrational anger would not arise unless sin were in your members; but take its rule away, let it not have weapons with which it may fight against you. It will learn, too, not to arise when it begins not to find weapons."[28] For Augustine, it is not only possible to restrain sinful ac-

---

23. Latin: "libertas plena atque perfecta." *In Johannis*, 365; *Tractates on the Gospel of John 28–54*, 148.

24. See *In Johannis*, 362.

25. See ibid., 363.

26. For an elaboration, see Nisula, *Augustine and the Functions of Concupiscence*, chap. 6.

27. See *In Johannis*, 363–64.

28. Latin: "Surgit ira? noli dare irae linguam ad maledicendum; . . . Non surgeret ira

tions; it is also possible to diminish sinful desires through ongoing spiritual discipline.

Throughout his exhortations, Augustine reminds his flock that they depend on grace in their continual struggle against sin. Using a therapeutic image to highlight the activity of grace, he states: "Just as a doctor hates the sickness of the sick man and in healing directs his effort so that the sickness be driven away and the sick man relieved, so God by his grace directs his effort in us, so that the sin be destroyed and the person set free."[29] Through the grace of the Physician a continually deeper healing from sin can take place, although a complete healing is reserved for the life to come.

Here it must be noted that the reason this healing remains incomplete is *not* because God is incapable of destroying all sin. Throughout the Pelagian controversy, Augustine consistently held that perfection in this life is a *possibility* due to divine sovereignty. However, in Augustine's view, healing remains incomplete so that believers will remain humble and continually dependent on grace. As J. Patout Burns notes, "Augustine explained that God allows Christians to continue experiencing their weakness . . . in order to prevent a resurgence of the pride and self-reliance which caused the original fall of humanity. A lesser grace is given so that a greater sin may be forestalled."[30]

In summary, Augustine's vision of sanctification, as evidenced in selections from his sermons on John, centers on the believer's participation in Christ. The fully divine incarnate Son has made possible a real transformation of sinful human beings. Augustine explains this transformation with many metaphors—regeneration, healing, renewal of the image of God, adoption, and deification. This transformation depends utterly on God's initiative. By grace God took on human nature, and by grace individuals are conformed to Christ and made participants in the divine nature. Although sanctification will be complete only in the life to come, the believer can make genuine progress in sanctity with the aid of grace. Encouraging that progress in sanctity is one of the primary agendas of Augustine's preaching.

---

ista irrationabilis, nisi peccatum esset in membris; sed tolle illi regnum, non habeat arma unde contra te pugnet; discet etiam non surgere, cum arma coeperit non invenire." *In Johannis*, 364; *Tractates on the Gospel of John 28–54*, 147.

29. Latin: "Quomodo odit medicus aegritudinem aegroti, et id agit curando ut aegritudo pellatur, aeger levetur, sic Deus gratia sua hoc in nobis agit, ut peccatum consumatur, homo liberetur." *In Johannis*, 362–63; *Tractates on the Gospel of John 28–54*, 145.

30. Burns, "Grace," 397.

The Sufficiency of Christ: Wesley on Sanctification

As a renewal movement within the eighteenth-century Church of England, the primary purpose of Methodism, according to John Wesley, was to "spread scriptural holiness over the land."[31] Wesley and the early Methodists were committed to a robust vision of human transformation under grace. According to Wesley, this transformation begins in justification and new birth and continues throughout the believer's life. The extent of this transformation is expressed in the doctrine of Christian perfection or entire sanctification, which holds that human beings, in this life, can be completely without sin and made perfect in love.[32]

Similar to Augustine, Wesley's vision of holiness centers on the person of Christ and his work in the economy of salvation. This can be seen particularly in his 1781 sermon "The End of Christ's Coming," which is a commentary on 1 John 3:8: "For this purpose was the Son of God manifested, that he might destroy the works of the devil." In this sermon, Wesley locates the reality of sanctification within the broader story of creation, fall, and redemption. Created in the image of God, human beings were endowed with understanding, will, and freedom (that is, the "natural image"), as well as "righteousness and true holiness" (that is, "the moral image").[33] In his original state, man enjoyed union with the Trinity: "he was unspeakably happy, dwelling in God and God in him, having an uninterrupted fellowship with the Father and the Son through the eternal Spirit."[34] However, through the devil evil entered into the creation. Tempted by the devil, Adam and Eve turned away from God in unbelief, pride, and self-will. The result of their sin was that the natural image (understanding, will, and freedom) was impaired; the entire moral image (righteousness and holiness) was destroyed; and fellowship with the Trinity was lost.

Having narrated the story of creation and fall, Wesley then describes how the Son was manifested to destroy the works of the devil. These works are "sin and its fruits."[35] Wesley identifies different manifestations of the Son. The Son was revealed first to the angels in his equality with the Father before the world's creation and then to the patriarchs of the old covenant.

---

31. Wesley, "Minutes of Several Conversations," 299.
32. For a nuanced treatment of the doctrine, see Abraham, "Christian Perfection."
33. Wesley, "The End of Christ's Coming," 475.
34. Ibid., 475–76.
35. Ibid., 477.

The greatest manifestation of the Son was his incarnation, ministry, and sacrificial death followed by his resurrection, ascension, and outpouring of the Holy Spirit. Wesley moves seamlessly from these past manifestations of the Son to the Son's present manifestation in the human heart. The Son is manifested inwardly, first, to destroy unbelief by empowering one to believe in him. This denotes justification by faith, which entails a restoration of peace with God. Second, the Son is manifested inwardly to destroy pride and self-will. This signals entire sanctification or the renewal of the moral image. It includes deliverance from sin, specifically "the desire of the flesh, the desire of the eyes, and the pride of life" (1 John 2:16). In destroying these works of the devil, the Son brings about nothing less than "real religion," which Wesley describes as "a restoration of man, by him that bruises the serpent's head, to all that the old serpent deprived him of; a restoration not only to the favour, but likewise to the image of God; implying not barely deliverance from sin but the being filled with the fullness of God."[36]

Like Augustine, then, Wesley holds that the Son has made possible a real transformation of sinful human beings. Through his incarnation, death, and resurrection as well as his present work in the heart, the Son restores human beings to peace with God, renews within them the image of their Creator, and grants them a share in God's own life. There is for Wesley, however, a limit to the transformation effected by the Son: "The Son of God does not destroy the whole work of the devil in man, as long as he remains in this life."[37] Wesley notes that those renewed in righteousness and true holiness will remain subject to the infirmities of the corruptible body (pain, sickness, weakness of understanding, and so on) until the Son is manifested to destroy death itself. However, Wesley concludes this 1781 sermon by reminding his audience of the great depth of transformation that is possible *here and now*:

> Be not content with any religion which does not imply the destruction of all the works of the devil, that is, of all sin. We know weakness of understanding, and a thousand infirmities, will remain... But sin need not remain: this is the work of the devil, eminently so called, which the Son of God was manifested to destroy in this present life. He is able, he is willing, to destroy it now in all that believe in him.[38]

---

36. Ibid., 482.
37. Ibid.
38. Ibid., 483.

As can be seen from this quotation, Wesley's belief in entire sanctification in this life is grounded in nothing other than his belief in the sufficiency of God in Christ. The Son of God is able and willing to destroy all sin and restore complete righteousness and holiness to the one who has faith in him.

Augustine and Wesley: Preachers of Sanctification

By way of comparison, I would like to identify two broad consistencies and one important variance between Augustine and Wesley's respective visions of holiness. First, Augustine and Wesley offer a vision of holiness that begins with what God has done in Christ in the economy of salvation. In Augustine's sermons on John, the incarnation of the Word is the greatest instance of grace whereby God participated in human nature so that human beings could participate in God. Likewise, Wesley roots his understanding of sanctification in the mission of the Son in human history. Through Christ's life, death, and resurrection as well as his ongoing work in the human heart, God has acted powerfully and effectively to defeat evil and restore human beings to union with the Trinity. Augustine and Wesley provide a theocentric—more specifically, a Christocentric—account of sanctification.[39] For both preachers, claims about sanctification are rooted firmly in the doctrines of God and Christ.

Second, Augustine and Wesley offer a vision of holiness that emphasizes real transformation in the life of the believer. Both figures can describe this transformation in terms of participation in God's nature.[40] For Augustine, this transformation begins with the grace of baptism and is deepened as the believer resists sinful desires with the help of divine grace. Augustine's stress on human transformation calls into question the traditional assumption that his vision of the Christian life is fundamentally unhopeful. Much like Wesley's, Augustine's vision upholds the necessity and possibility of dramatic growth in holiness. This growth involves genuine union with God. It depends on grace, but it also requires human participation. To the

39. This theocentric account could also be traced by looking at the vital role of the Holy Spirit in each figure's account of sanctification, a point stressed on the Wesleyan side by Kenneth Loyer's chapter in this volume.

40. For example, Wesley states that sanctification is "the life of God in the soul of man; a participation of the divine nature; the mind that was in Christ; or, the renewal of our heart, after the image of him that created us" (Journal Entry, "13 September 1739," 97). For a discussion of the theme of participation in Wesley, see Maddox, *Responsible Grace*, esp. 178.

point, Augustine states, "as believers, participating in his grace, enlightened by him, we are in him, and he is in us."[41]

Finally, let me specify the variance. Although Augustine emphasizes a real change that comes from the believer's participation in Christ, for him the Christian life is marked by a continual "warfare" against sin.[42] No matter the degree of transformation, the Christian is engaged in an ongoing struggle against concupiscence. Augustine views this struggle as a "means of grace," for it makes the believer depend on God and therefore prevents pride.[43]

Yet from a Wesleyan perspective, the claim that believers have to struggle continually against sin so as not to fall into pride seems misplaced. For if holiness consists in conformity to Christ, as Wesley often articulates it, then it would include conformity to Christ's *humility*. In his 1784 sermon "On Perfection," Wesley stresses that Christian Perfection entails having the very mind of Christ. Having the very mind of Christ "*immediately* and *directly* refers to the humility of our Lord, yet it may be taken in a far more extensive sense, so as to include the whole disposition of his mind, all his affections, all his tempers, both toward God and man."[44] Thus, while Augustine has a robust notion of the Christian life as union with and participation in Christ, Wesley takes this notion to its logical conclusion. In entire sanctification, Christians are so deeply united to Christ and so transformed into his likeness that they come to share in Christ's humble disposition. This conviction of Wesley calls into question the Augustinian notion that perfection in this life inevitably leads to pride.

---

41. Latin: "fideles participantes eius gratiam, illuminati ab ipso, in illo sumus, et ipse in nobis." *In Johannis*, 418; *Tractates on the Gospel of John 28–54*, 236.

42. "The life of the just in this body is still a warfare, not a triumphal celebration" (*Sermons on the New Testament 148–183*, 40). In contrast, Wesley holds that in entire sanctification love fills the person to the point that "there is no mixture of any contrary affections—all is peace and harmony" ("On Patience," 176).

43. See Burnell, "Concupiscence and Moral Freedom in Augustine and before Augustine," 60.

44. Wesley, "On Perfection," 74; emphasis mine. In "A Plain Account of the People Called Methodists," Wesley states that, since the beginning of the movement, the Methodists have insisted that true "religion" (that is, holiness) is "nothing short of or different from 'the mind that was in Christ'" (255).

Conclusion

In this chapter, I have attempted to show that, when it comes to the theme of holiness, the common ground between Augustine and Wesley is more expansive than either Wesley himself or his modern interpreters have supposed. When viewed as preachers, we find that Augustine and Wesley shared a fervent desire to see those under their spiritual care grow in holiness. They faithfully preached the scriptures to that end. Yet their preaching on holiness did not primarily consist of exhortations toward moral improvement. Above all, as we have seen, their sermons centered on God and his work in the economy of salvation. In light of that work, Augustine and Wesley consistently highlighted for their listeners the *hopeful* possibility of real transformation in Christ. They preached that Christian existence entails a continually deepened union with Christ and participation in his divine life. However, Wesley held that this union with Christ goes all the way down; it entails conformity to Christ's own humble mind. Herein lies Wesley's distinct contribution: a thoroughly Christocentric vision of holiness that challenges the Augustinian tradition's anxiety about perfection and pride. Simply put, if holiness is truly union with Christ, then holiness entails humility.

As Wesleyan scholars seek to identify Wesley's distinct voice within the church catholic, two broader observations are in order in light of the foregoing analysis. First, fruitful interactions can be had between Wesley and other figures when we view the theme of holiness more directly in relation to doctrines of God, Christ, and the Spirit, as opposed to viewing holiness solely under the rubric of the Christian life. Second, it is constructive to look at homiletical works when comparing Wesley to figures from the Christian past, particularly the church fathers. Like Wesley, preaching was a central task of the church fathers. Like Wesley, the sermons of the fathers were theological works in their own right. Homiletical works provide a significant point of contact between Wesley and his forebears and fertile ground for constructive analyses of Wesley's place within the church catholic.

6

"The Complete Art of Happiness"
Listening to the Sermon on the Mount with Wesley and Aquinas

Edgardo Colón-Emeric

"THE DAY OF THE Great Fiesta." This is how the "Hispanic Creed" describes the coming kingdom.[1] Heaven is a happy place. Its citizens are called *beati*, "happy ones." The pilgrims who cross the Jordan are greeted by the beatific vision, the happy sight, of the New Jerusalem, a city decorated for a wedding party. The celebratory character of the kingdom is vouchsafed by strict standards for admission. In the parable of the wedding banquet, one of the guests is kicked out for not wearing a wedding garment (see Matt 22:12), which Wesley interprets to mean that the guest was not clothed in holiness.[2] If Wesley is right, and I think he is, then the chief qualification for being a celestial party animal is being a saint. This is very odd indeed. Holiness seems to be all about saying "no, no, no" whereas happiness seems to be about "yes, yes, yes." There are many adjectives that come to mind when thinking of the heroes of the faith, but fun is probably not one of these. I love John Wesley, but would I really like to have him over for a Fourth of July picnic? Leaving aside the fact that he was a Tory and that

---

1. *Mil Voces para Celebrar*, 70.
2. See Wesley, "On the Wedding Garment."

he opposed the independence of the colonies, would not his discipline of holy conversation dampen the mood around the barbecue grill? Holiness appears to consist in self-denial, happiness in self-realization. Which is it? In typical Wesleyan fashion, the answer is "both." Happiness and holiness are tied together. "The day of the great fiesta" is the day of our final sanctification.

In this essay, I would like to consider the conjunction of happiness and holiness by listening to the Sermon on the Mount, and in particular to the Beatitudes, with hearing aids borrowed from John Wesley and Thomas Aquinas. My selection of theologians is not haphazard. Whatever their limitations, these two theologians carry tremendous weight within their respective traditions. In a previous study, I considered the doctrine of perfection in Wesley and Aquinas.[3] I argued for the commonality of the content of their theology and for the complementarity of their methodology. I believe that the conjunction of the Anglican evangelist and the Dominican preacher into a Wesleyan-Thomism offers a fruitful way for Methodists to engage in Christian theology in the twenty-first century. Reading the Thomistic and Wesleyan gloss on the gospel of Matthew is an exercise in ecumenical Biblical hermeneutics. Looking over the shoulders of Aquinas and Wesley as they read Scripture can help us become better students of its author. The goal of this hermeneutical exercise is not simply comparative but constructive—to illuminate the connection between holiness and happiness.

The selection of texts is not accidental. John Wesley dedicated thirteen of his forty-four Standard Sermons to a patient, careful exposition of this greatest of all sermons, whereas Thomas Aquinas lectured on the Sermon on the Mount at the University of Paris where he served as *magister in sacra pagina* ("teacher of the sacred page"). Thomas also gave the Beatitudes a structural role in the second part of the *Summa Theologiae* where the desire for beatitude marks the launching point for the human's journey to God. In other words, for both Wesley and Aquinas, the Beatitudes played a central role in their understanding of how God sanctified the human. I hope that by listening to Jesus with the help of Wesley and Aquinas we learn a little more about "the complete art of happiness."[4]

---

3. Colón-Emeric, *Wesley, Aquinas, and Christian Perfection*.
4. Wesley, *Explanatory Notes upon the New Testament*, 28.

Overview of Interpretation History of the Sermon on the Mount

Throughout history, Christians have turned to Matthew 5 through 7 for guidance and inspiration in describing the baptized life. The Sermon on the Mount loomed large in the thought of patristic and scholastic authors who admired the sublimity of its content while wondering how to scale its seemingly inaccessible heights. A running question has been, Who can keep up with the demands of this sermon? Answers to this question have varied over the centuries, but many have sought to soften its demands. Thomist theologian Servais Pinckaers sketches five typical interpretive strategies that each in its own way relieves Christians of the burden of building their lives on this mount.[5]

1. *The dualist interpretation.* This reading, typically associated with Roman Catholicism, interprets the Sermon on the Mount as moral instruction for a spiritual elite committed to attaining Christian perfection. Jesus is speaking here to the twelve disciples who have left everything behind (families, homes, work) in order to follow him. The Sermon on the Mount can only be kept by those who have climbed a Monte Cassino or Mount Athos; its true audience would be monks and nuns. Only someone who has untied all manner of personal and social bonds has a chance at living into the message of this homily. By contrast, the summit of ordinary Christian discipleship is found in the Ten Commandments. Any violation of Moses' Decalogue is a mortal sin but going against the Sermon is a minor offense since for the average Christian, its message is optional.

2. *The dialectical interpretation.* This reading, typically associated with Lutheran traditions, presents the Sermon on the Mount as law. The purpose of this sermon is to demonstrate the impossibility of being justified by the law. Jesus preaches the impossible so that we will cling to him all the more fiercely. If one is looking for guidance to Christian life, one needs to turn to the Epistle to the Romans and its message of justification by faith. Jesus needs to be read through Paul and not vice versa. In short, only Christ can fulfill the imperatives of this sermon. His obedience takes the place of ours.

3. *The idealist interpretation.* This interpretation became common among mainline Protestants. The Sermon on the Mount presents us with an ideal. This ideal is unachievable and yet not altogether lacking in practical utility. The Sermon presents a perfect goal that we will never attain,

---

5. Pinckaers, *The Sources of Christian Ethics*, 135–39.

but at least it provides our efforts with a direction. Also, the Sermon on the Mount teaches us that Christianity, in distinction from Judaism, is an inward religion—what really matters are not our actions but our dispositions and feelings.

4. *The apocalyptic interpretation.* Albert Schweitzer interpreted the Sermon on the Mount as an interim ethic. The manner of life announced by Jesus made sense for people who looked for the imminent return of the Messiah. The strict moral injunctions expressed in Matthew's gospel are similar to those of other apocalyptic communities of antiquity and modernity. For primitive Christians it made sense to share earthly goods (see Acts 4:32), promise virginity (1 Cor 7), and accept martyrdom (2 Tim 4:6) because they believed that Jesus was about to return. But with the passing of decades, centuries, and millennia, the Sermon on the Mount loses its flavor and relevance.

5. *The social interpretation.* For Leo Tolstoy, the Sermon on the Mount offers a social program for a better world. The teachings of Jesus present us a blueprint for building the kingdom of God on earth. This interpretation is favored by liberation theologians for whom the Sermon on the Mount is a political manifesto that encourages concrete social action. Some theologians actually favor the Lukan version of the Sermon which includes condemnation of the rich ("Woe to you who are rich!") over the Matthean declaration of happiness for the "poor in spirit."

Each of these strands of interpretation contributes to our understanding of the shape of Christian discipleship. Following Jesus does have social consequences, it is apocalyptic, it is dialectical, and it does allow for stars of greater and lesser glory. However, considered in isolation, these interpretations offer a myopic view of the Christian life presented in Jesus' sermon. With this background in mind, I now consider how Wesley reads the Sermon on the Mount and in particular the Beatitudes.

Listening with Wesley to the Sermon on the Mount

In a span of seven years, John Wesley preached over a hundred sermons on the Sermon on the Mount, amounting to just over one sermon a month.[6] Wesley was captivated by the difficulty and promise of Jesus' master homily. The thirteen discourses on the Sermon on the Mount which were included in his collection of *Sermons on Several Occasions* were composed

6. See Outler's introductory comments to Wesley's series of sermons in *WJW* 1:467.

between 1748 and 1750. To understand the import of these sermons, two observations are to be kept in mind regarding their composition. First, the sermons were composed at a time when Wesley was beginning to integrate the traditional teachings on sanctification which he had inherited from his Anglican forebears (particularly William Law and Jeremy Taylor) with the fresh insights he gained about the doctrine of justification from his encounters with the Moravians. Second, these sermons should also be read against the background of rationalism and industrialism in eighteenth century England.[7] In these sermons, Wesley is preaching a way of life that challenges deism on the one hand and materialism on the other. As such, the thirteen discourses on the Sermon on the Mount can and should be read as a significant piece of moral theology. In Thomistic parlance, this collection of sermons constitutes a mini *Secunda Pars*, a short summation of the creature's journey to God. In this regard, the placement of this sermon series within the Wesleyan published sermon corpus where it follows the sermon "The Lord Our Righteousness" is significant. As Steve Long states, "Only after Wesley has explained Christ's righteousness by explicit references to the doctrine of the Trinity and the Incarnation, and after explaining how this righteousness is not simply imputed to us but also inherent in us, can he then show us the shape of this righteousness."[8]

The Sermon on the Mount is Wesley's answer to Anselm's question: *Cur Deus homo?* Why did God become human? Wesley elaborates, "To bless them, to make men happy, was the great business for which our Lord came into the world. And accordingly He here pronounces eight blessings together, annexing them to so many steps in Christianity."[9] For Wesley, the Sermon on the Mount is nothing less than a roadmap to happiness, a happiness to which Jesus calls all humankind. After all, if the message were intended only for the spiritual elite of the twelve, then why did Jesus climb to the top of the Mount of Olives to speak in front of a multitude? Wesley dismisses the objections of those who claim that the hard parts of the sermon are only applicable to the apostles and the primitive church. No, says Wesley, "either all the parts of this discourse are to be applied to men in general, or no part; seeing they are all connected together, all joined as the

---

7. See broadly Meistad, *Martin Luther and John Wesley on the Sermon on the Mount*, 86–87.

8. Long, *John Wesley's Moral Theology*, 141.

9. *Explanatory Notes upon the New Testament*, 28.

stones in an arch, of which you cannot take one away, without destroying the whole fabric."[10]

Jesus begins his sermon with the Beatitudes and Wesley's exposition does likewise.

The Beatitudes are the most perfect description of Christianity. In these words, we see "a picture of God, so far as he is imitable by man! A picture drawn by God's own hand!"[11] Following longstanding tradition and also his knowledge of the Greek New Testament, Wesley interprets the proclamations of "blessed" as declarations of happiness (*makarioi*). In studying this sermon, Wesley hopes to transcribe the contours of the divine figure traced by the eight declarations of happiness into the hearts of his readers. In order to attain this goal, Wesley first considers the pattern of the Beatitudes. Each of the Beatitudes praises a holy temper as happy and offers a reason for this happiness. What is a holy temper?

The language of tempers is part and parcel of eighteenth century moral theology. Tempers are enduring inclinations or dispositions. The tempers are related to emotions but the constancy of their power distinguishes them from the transitory movement of the latter. Emotions come and go. Hearing a news story might move me to anger, but the next one might move me to pity. The tempers are more stable. They denote character-traits like patience, courage, and humility. The tempers are a key term in Wesley's moral lexicon. "True religion," says Wesley, "is right tempers towards God and man."[12] The right tempers are holy tempers.

The holy tempers are seeds of grace sown in human nature. Holy tempers make it possible for holy actions to blossom from holy affections. Changing metaphors, the holy tempers are the moral muscles that keep the human upright in their walk with and to God. They are strengthened through exercise and they atrophy from disuse. Some holy tempers can be described as "passive graces"[13] or "passive virtues."[14] These tempers are strengthened by experiences of suffering. Wesley remarks, "By occasion of this [children of God] attained many holy tempers which otherwise could have no being: resignation to God, confidence in him in times of trouble and danger, patience, meekness, longsuffering, and the whole train of pas-

---

10. Wesley, "Upon Our Lord's Sermon on the Mount, I," 473.
11. Wesley, "Upon Our Lord's Sermon on the Mount, III," 530.
12. Wesley, "The Unity of Divine Being," 66.
13. Wesley, "God's Love to Fallen Man," 429.
14. Ibid., 432.

sive virtues."[15] Other tempers, like benevolence, pertain more to the activity and the life of good works. In either case, whether passive or active, the whole train of tempers is guided to its end by love. Love heals the affections and is the sole principle that orients the tempers to the mind of Christ.[16]

In terms of the Sermon on the Mount, Wesley teaches that the divine tempers praised in the Beatitudes are not reserved for the few; rather, "both poverty of spirit, and every other temper which is here mentioned, are at all times found, in a greater or less degree, in every real Christian."[17] The difference between the mediocre Christian and the saint of God is not in the sower or the seeds but in the soil. The seeds of grace have been sown in all, but not all cultivate the tempers and so for this reason many Christians remain fruitless. Switching metaphors again, without exercise our moral muscles remain flabby and weak. Exercise of the tempers is key to their growth. But different tempers are stimulated by different exercises. For example, the temper of meekness is strengthened by ministering to the poor. Conversely, this same temper atrophies by growing in riches. As the tempers grow in strength through their exercise, we grow in holiness, and as we grow in holiness, we grow in happiness. Wesley's description of the Beatitudes as "the complete art of happiness" is apt. Happiness takes practice.

Wesley read the Sermon on the Mount as more than a collection of sayings. It was not, so to speak, a "Saturday night special" prepared in haste. Rather, Jesus had plenty of preparation time for its preaching: the forty days in the wilderness, the years in Nazareth, the centuries of walking with Israel, and an eternity of triune living. Wesley considered this sermon to have been composed in the very heart of God, and thus there is nothing accidental about its composition, delivery, or redaction.

The Beatitudes do not compose a random list of proverbs but an ordered whole. Each of the Beatitudes is ordered toward the goal of union with God. Each marks a step on the road to perfect happiness. Every temper builds upon the other. The "poor in spirit" are those who recognize their sin and humble themselves in repentance. Poverty of spirit is also "a continual sense of our total dependence on him for every good thought or word or work."[18] Poverty of spirit is then the first step on the way to salvation and also an abiding characteristic of the saved. The Beatitudes are

15. Ibid.
16. Wesley, "The New Birth," 188.
17. Wesley, "Upon Our Lord's Sermon on the Mount, I," 479.
18. Ibid., 482.

ordered toward each other and are mutually reinforcing.[19] For instance, the sense of dependence made possible by poverty of spirit is indispensable for purity of heart.

The exercise of the holy tempers encounters resistance in this life. On the one hand, holiness is hindered by bad habits like judging others. On the other hand, holiness is hindered by bad examples of holiness. Wesley concludes his exposition of the Sermon on the Mount by reflecting on the story of the one who builds his house on the sand and the one who builds on the rock. By means of this contrast, Wesley calls all his readers to engage in self-examination, and he exhorts them to exercise the holy tempers so as to attain the happiness promised in the Beatitudes.

Listening with Aquinas to the Sermon on the Mount

Thomas Aquinas lectured on the Sermon on the Mount as part of his teaching in Paris during the years 1269 and 1270.[20] The dating is disputed, but if correct, it points to a turbulent period for Aquinas when the Dominican way of life was threatened by foes in the academy and the church hierarchy. What attracted Thomas to the Dominicans was the conjunction of love of poverty and love of learning. The *Ordo Praedicatorum* was established by Domingo de Guzmán (1170–1221) in 1216 in order to combat the Cathar heresy. They were the "hounds of God," the *Domini-canes*, who fought against heresy with the bark of their preaching. Unlike the monks, the mendicants were an urban movement. The latter took vows of poverty rather than the monastic vows of stability. For these friars, begging was a way of life. In their case, the Dominicans received a special dispensation from canonical prayers for study (*vita mixta*) for the sake of their mission. As a Dominican, then, Aquinas encountered in the Sermon on the Mount the supreme exposition of the *doctrina Christi* and the confirmation of the Dominican way of life, which begins in poverty, grows in contemplation, and ends in action.

Aquinas's teaching on the Sermon on the Mount begins with the discussion of a theological axiom: *omnes enim homines appetunt beatitudinem*.[21] "All humans hunger for happiness." The human predicament is that people look for happiness in all the wrong places. Jesus' preaching begins

---

19. Wesley, "Upon Our Lord's Sermon on the Mount, II," 498.
20. See broadly Torrell, *Saint Thomas Aquinas*, 56.
21. Aquinas, *Lectura super Mattheum* 5.2.

with the Beatitudes in order to rectify this situation. Jesus announces that the poor in spirit are happy in order to correct those who look for happiness in the possession of material things. Against those who delight in payback, Jesus says happy are the meek. Against those who set their hopes on the *dolce vita*, he declares happy are those who weep. To those who pursue happiness in the desert, he cautions eschatological reserve: the pure in heart *shall* see God. To those who look for meaning and purpose in the life of active service, he tells them the peacemakers are happy not on account of their success but because of what God has promised that they are going to be called: children of God. In preaching the Beatitudes Jesus diagnoses our sickened adherence to worldly happiness and frees us for attaining the end of true happiness: union with God by knowledge and love.

The happiness announced in the Beatitudes consists of virtuous acts. For Aquinas, happiness is nothing else than the fulfilling of one's purpose with excellence and ease. One might say that happiness is a verb, a verb that can be conjugated in two modalities: common and heroic. Consider for instance the declaration of poverty in the first beatitude. One can be poor by necessity or by humility. Only the latter's voluntary detachment from earthly goods pertains to virtue and happiness. However, there are two modalities of detachment. There is the detachment practiced by those who have riches but do not become spiritually entangled by them. This poverty of spirit pertains to common virtue and happiness. There is also detachment practiced by those who forsake riches and embrace poverty. This practice of detachment is superhuman or heroic in degree, and it is this degree of virtue and happiness that is the object of the Beatitudes. Every Christian is fertile soil for the heroic happiness of the Beatitudes, but only in mature Christians can we see the first shoots of this lovely tree.[22] The happiness announced in the Beatitudes begins on earth, but its final consummation is eschatological.

The Angelic Doctor, like Wesley, reads the Beatitudes as more than a laundry list of meritorious virtues. The Beatitudes depend on each other. Poverty of spirit is not sufficient for beatitude. Meekness is needed to temper anger toward the rich or envy of their wealth.[23] Hunger for justice without mercy will not lead to happiness because "justice without mercy is cruelty, and mercy without justice is the mother of debauchery."[24] Like the

---

22. *ST*, 1—2.69.2 (2:886–87).
23. *Lectura super Mattheum* 5.2.
24. Ibid.

fingers of the hand, virtues grow proportionally.[25] Therefore even though it is true that some saints are more renowned for the practice of one virtue or another, there is no room for specialization in moral theology in the sense that some virtues are simply ignored for the sake of others. A person with perfect justice but no mercy would not be a saint but a caricature of a person, indeed a monster (think of Inspector Javert in Victor Hugo's *Les Misérables*). Only when the virtues are united in a harmonious ensemble can we speak of perfect virtue and Christian perfection.

The Beatitudes are ordered in terms of the promised reward. Aquinas finds the reason for this ordering in the nature of virtue itself. Virtues serve a threefold purpose. First, virtues withdraw our desires from harmful or evil things. The humility of spiritual poverty, the tears that accompany mourning, and the mercy of those who have received mercy all heal the soul from its attachment to cupidity and cruelty. Second, virtues dispose one to good acts. Hunger and thirst for justice impel one to act justly and to work for justice. Third, virtues incline one to what is best—to know and love God.[26] The Beatitudes are ordered toward the rewards of seeing God and being called children of God. The seventh beatitude is the culmination of the first six because peacemaking is associated with the seventh day of creation, the day of rest and peace. One might expect the Beatitudes to end at this point with the Sabbath, but for the Christian, the resurrection of Christ on the first day of the week inaugurates a new creation. And just as the promised reward of the eighth day is greater than that of the seventh, the eighth beatitude is the perfection of all other beatitudes. The eighth beatitude proclaims the happiness of the martyr who receives the reward of the kingdom of heaven. The martyrs share this reward with the poor in spirit, but there are two differences. First, the poor in spirit receive the kingdom of heaven as a reward for their humility, but the martyrs do so for their charity. Second, for the poor in spirit the reward is received in hope, but for the martyrs it is in reality.

One of the features of Aquinas's interpretation of the Beatitudes which surely strikes contemporary readers as odd is the way in which Thomas correlates the Beatitudes with the gifts and fruit of the Spirit. Aquinas interweaves Isaiah 11:2 ("the spirit of wisdom and understanding, the spirit of counsel and might, the spirit of knowledge and the fear of the LORD") and Galatians 5:22–23 ("the fruit of the Spirit is love, joy, peace, patience,

---

25. *ST*, 1—2.66.1 (2:865–66).
26. *Lectura super Mattheum* 5.2.

kindness, generosity, faithfulness, gentleness, and self-control"). The correlation, though not original to Aquinas (it was also proposed by Augustine) is systematically developed in the *Summa Theologiae*. The Angelic Doctor does not believe that the theological virtues of faith, hope, and love are self-sustaining; they need the support of the gifts of the Spirit. When these gifts are in operation, the theological virtues yield the fruit of the Spirit which blossoms in the Beatitudes. Faith needs to be perfected by the gift of understanding. Hope is perfected by the gift of the fear of the Lord and is associated with the beatitude of spiritual poverty. Love cannot be made perfect without the gift of wisdom, which renders us peacemakers. The correlation might seem exegetically forced, yet it is theologically accurate. It is by means of this correlation that Thomas draws the connections between the shape of the Christian life as preached by Jesus and taught by Paul with the life of Christ as prophesied by Isaiah. In reading these texts together, Aquinas defends the supernatural character and Christocentric orientation of the Christian life. The happy one, par excellence, is Jesus Christ, whose life, death, and resurrection make possible creation's attainment of final felicity.

Teachers of Scripture

John Wesley and Thomas Aquinas were preachers. Scripture was their primary theological text. Aquinas was a *magister in sacra pagina*. Wesley was a *homo unius libri*. Both privileged the literal meaning of the text. Both read Scripture in conversation with the Church Fathers. Wesley, more than Aquinas, endeavored to avoid the use of non-biblical language. His reverence for the words of Scripture and his desire to be plain-spoken made him cautious in his use of non-biblical terminology. For instance, Wesley did not insist on the use of the word "Trinity" by Christians because the term, valuable as it was, did not appear in Scripture.[27] Despite this reticence, Wesley returned time and again to the language of the tempers in order to elucidate the promise and challenge of the Sermon on the Mount. Ultimately, Wesley (like Aquinas) understood that philosophy could be a

---

27. Wesley, "On the Trinity," 377: "I dare not insist upon anyone's using the word 'Trinity' or 'Person.' I use them myself without any scruple, because I know of none better. But if any man has any scruple concerning them, who shall constrain him to use them? I cannot."

helpful walking stick supporting our little faith as we seek to ascend the sublime heights of God's wisdom.

The ways in which Wesley and Aquinas read the Sermon on the Mount cannot be easily tied to the interpretive strands catalogued by Pinckaers. To be sure, there are threads of elitism in Thomas' reading and patterns of social reform in Wesley's, but their interpretation appears in general to be cut from a different cloth. "Wesley does to the ancient virtue tradition precisely what Aquinas himself did when he made infused virtue the essence of the moral life. Virtue is no longer a human achievement, an *arete* or heroic power. Neither Achilles nor Socrates is the paradigm of virtue. Little room remains for Aristotle's 'great-souled man,' who remains untouched by the passions of those beneath him."[28] Both read the Sermon on the Mount Christologically. For Wesley, the Beatitudes are "a picture of God, so far as he is imitable by man! A picture drawn by God's own hand!"[29] For Aquinas, the Beatitudes are the fulfillment of the prophecy of Isaiah 11:2, "The spirit of the LORD shall rest on him." The Beatitudes are the best portrait we have of Jesus.[30] Jesus is the one who is poor in spirit, who mourns for us and for our salvation, who is meek and lowly in heart, and who hungers and thirsts for justice. Jesus is the one who is so pure in heart that he can freely approach the throne of grace; he is the merciful one, the peacemaker, and for all these reasons, he is the one who is persecuted.

"The Complete Art of Happiness"

In the Sermon on the Mount, Jesus offers humanity what Wesley called "the complete art of happiness." The term sounds odd to modern ears, but what Wesley wants to say is that happiness is not something that simply happens to us; it is something we do. "People become lighter as they become stronger. As great artists perform with seeming effortlessness and can enjoy the beauty of their own artistry, people become happier as they love more supplely, enskilled by divine wisdom."[31] Happiness is a word whose moral worth is inadequately appreciated. Christians have too often abandoned this word to the self-help section of the bookstore. Repeatedly, theological ethics is based on the utilitarian calculus of the needs of the many or on the

---

28. Long, *John Wesley's Moral Theology*, 146.
29. Wesley, "Upon Our Lord's Sermon on the Mount, III," 530.
30. See broadly Cantalamessa, *Beatitudes*, 35–36.
31. Charry, *God and the Art of Happiness*, 277.

obligation of doing the right thing. Wesley and Aquinas, on the contrary, would have us base our common life on happiness. Both would support the work of contemporary theological ethicists like Paul Wadell who describe Christian morality as "training in happiness."[32] The word "happiness" must be rescued from its counterfeits inside and outside the church. It is too important a term to let it be defined by prosperity preachers and life-coaches. There is a craft to happiness, and it takes practice to make it perfect. Aquinas and Wesley help us to identify key features of this art.

1. *Happiness is not simply an emotion but an act.* Happiness consists in accomplishing the purpose of our existence with excellence and ease. For rocks, happiness means lying around being solid. For water, happiness means flowing smoothly and clearly. For a horse, happiness is galloping on an open field with other horses. For the human, happiness is union with God. The cosmos unfolds as a play in two perfect acts. The first act of the human drama begins with being made after the image of God. Beatitude is a perfect second act, a virtuous act, the noblest deed whereby humans are united to God by knowledge and love.[33] Human history is ultimately a divine comedy.

2. *Happiness is an act of affirmation.* It has been said that "what distinguishes the Christian martyr is that he never utters a word against God's creation."[34] Happiness is an act of assent to creation and its creator. Yes, the world is real and good. Yes, in spite of all appearances to the contrary, life is beautiful. Our first response to another creature is gladness at its very existence. For Aquinas, the capacity of this affirmation is embedded in the structure of the human being. For Wesley, it is the gift of prevenient grace. But for both the Angelic Doctor and for Wesley, this affirmation has profound consequences for Christian life.

3. *Happiness is the fundamental human vocation.* Wesley and Aquinas interpret the Beatitudes via a broadly Aristotelian framework that posits happiness as that which all desire, yet their interpretation bursts the Athenian wineskins. Greek philosophers drew a sharp distinction between the happiness that belonged to the gods and the happiness available to humans. The Olympians alone were *makarioi*. The best that the Athenians could attain was *eudaimonia*, a pale shadow of the eternal bliss of Zeus. Even this

---

32. In Wadell's case, see *Happiness and the Christian Moral Life*, xv.

33. ST 3.2.10: "*unio sanctorum ad Deum [est] per cognitionem et amorem*" (see 4:2036).

34. Pieper, *In Tune with the World*, 21.

degree of happiness was only possible for the philosopher, a Socrates who dedicated himself to a life of leisure and study. By contrast, Wesley and Aquinas believe that humans ultimately desire nothing less than the happiness which is God's and that this is precisely what Jesus offers when he proclaims the poor in spirit to be *makarioi*.

4. *Happiness is inseparable from holiness.* Human existence is deeply paradoxical. The act which perfects human nature surpasses the capacities of human nature. Happiness requires a "principle within of watchful, godly fear."[35] This principle, which can only come as a gift of the Holy Spirit, Wesley calls a holy temper and Aquinas calls a virtue. But both agree that happiness flows from the actualization of these principles, imperfectly in this life yet fully in the life to come. We need the assistance of these holy habits to keep us steady on the narrow way that leads to everlasting life. We need the grace of the infused virtues to order, purify, and elevate our desires. Without the holy tempers we look for happiness in all the wrong places. Without poverty of spirit we confuse happiness with prosperity and obsess about the stock market. Without meekness we confuse happiness with security and base the sustainability of our way of life upon the protection of our borders. The pursuit of happiness and going on to perfection are one and the same journey.[36] Whether people know it or not, the longing for happiness is at the same time a longing for holiness. All are called to be poor in spirit. All are called to be meek, to be merciful, to be peacemakers, to endure persecution. All are called to the life of these evangelical virtues because all are called to be happy. All can be happy because God's grace has been copiously shed over humanity.

5. *Happiness is attainable in this life, only imperfectly.* On the one hand, the followers of Jesus are declared happy now. Jesus does not say that those who mourn *will* be happy when they are comforted in the sweet by and by. But happy *are* those who mourn. The Christian is "happy in the end and in the way; happy in this life and in life everlasting."[37] On the other hand, not all has been given. Not all has been revealed. Moreover, since happiness is linked to holiness, loss of holiness threatens happiness and vice

---

35. See Charles Wesley's hymn "I Want a Principle Within."

36. Wesley, "God's Love to Fallen Man," 431: "To sum up what has been said under this head. As the more holy we are upon earth the more happy we must be (seeing there is an inseparable connection between holiness and happiness); as the more good we do to others the more of present reward redounds in our own bosom; even as our sufferings for God lead us to 'rejoice' in him 'with joy unspeakable and full of glory.'"

37. Wesley, "Upon Our Lord's Sermon on the Mount, I," 474.

versa. Hence, in this life, just as there is no state of perfection beyond the possibility of falling into sin, there is no state of happiness secure from the possibility of misfortune. Most of the rewards in the Beatitudes are in the future tense, and even if Christians are declared happy now, this declaration is on the basis of hope, the virtue of the wayfarer. Perfect happiness awaits our landing on the eternal shores of heaven. The only ones who are truly happy or *beati* are the *sancti* above.

6. *Happiness is intrinsically social.* If, as Wesley says, there is no holiness but social holiness and happiness is inseparable from holiness, then we must conclude that there is no happiness but social happiness. Happiness is nurtured in and for community. When Jesus pronounces the Beatitudes, the word "happy" is plural in form: *makarioi*. The pursuit of happiness is not a solo journey but a mass pilgrimage. God seeks a happy people, and the chief means for rendering humans holy and happy is the church. Wesley and Aquinas believed that there is room within the church for intentional communities devoted to the pursuit of holiness. The religious orders whose integrity Aquinas vehemently defended were constituted as schools of perfection structured around the evangelical counsels of poverty, chastity, and obedience. Wesley organized his followers in societies of mutual accountability around the rules of discipleship. Both were hoping that their communities would serve as nurseries for sanctity where Christians learned that the "complete art of happiness" leads not to self-fulfillment but to self-emptying for the sake of the world. In this regard, the Great Commission of Matthew 28 cannot be understood in separation from the great sermon of Matthew 5–7. The command to "go to all the nations" also includes the instruction to "[teach] them to obey everything that I have commanded you," and both look back to the "happy are." The missiological mandate and its catechetical content have an anthropological foundation, a foundation succinctly expressed by the Aristotelian and Augustinian axiom: All human beings desire happiness.

The Day of the Great Fiesta

Happiness is the first word in the Sermon on the Mount and the dominant chord of Christianity. In their interpretation of the Beatitudes, Wesley and Aquinas challenge us to stretch our understanding of happiness. The felicity which Jesus promises does not entail a wholesale rejection of common notions of happiness, but their purification and elevation. The happiness I find in eating fine food, taking family vacations, and working at an exciting job is real, but by itself it is tattered and mismatched. Only in the saints do we find happiness and holiness fitting well. The *beati* are dressed for "the day of the Great Fiesta."

The problem with inviting people like Wesley or Aquinas to a picnic or barbecue is that they are so truly in tune with the world that we sound flat by comparison. Wesley, Aquinas, and all the saints really know how to party because they "find God alike in little things and in great."[38] Like Paul, they have learned to be content with what they have (see Phil 4:11). Like Chesterton they see no contradiction between a pint, a pipe, and a cross. The happiness of the saints is the cure for the vanity of the *dolce vita*. Their holiness is the cure for the pseudo-gravitas which weighs down our walk with God. Wesley and Aquinas learned the art of happiness from feasting on Jesus' word and flesh. And so I think it fitting to end by citing a Wesleyan hymn which describes the Eucharist, the chief means of holiness, as a pledge of heaven.[39]

> Happy the Souls to Jesus join'd,
> And sav'd by Grace alone,
> Walking in all thy Ways we find
> Our Heaven on Earth begun.
>
> The Church triumphant in thy Love
> Their mighty Joys we know,
> They sing the Lamb in Hymns above,
> And we in Hymns below.
>
> Thee in thy glorious Realm they praise,
> And bow before thy Throne,
> We in the Kingdom of thy Grace,
> The Kingdoms are but One.
>
> The Holy to the Holiest leads,
> From hence our Spirits rise,
> And He that in thy Statutes treads
> Shall meet Thee in the Skies.

---

38. Wesley, "The Life of Mr. Gregory Lopez," 414.
39. *HLS*, 83–84.

7

John Calvin and John Wesley on Sanctification

Stephen W. Rankin_____

A Fresh Look at a Familiar Argument

ONE OF THE MAJOR fault lines running through American Protestantism has been continuing disagreements between Calvinists and Wesleyans on various theological topics, like the scope of God's sovereignty and the accessibility of salvation. As often happens, the heirs of seminal Christian leaders contribute actively to their legacies and, over time, the ideas of the originators fade from the view of the wider Christian community. This process sometimes blurs important distinctions and overdraws differences. Don Thorsen's recent book on John Calvin and John Wesley, written from a Wesleyan perspective, offers an irenic corrective to a number of popular misunderstandings.[1]

The present chapter aims at a similar purpose of comparing Calvin and Wesley but with a narrower scope. We will focus on their visions of the goal of the Christian life, that is, on sanctification. In the process, we will take as conciliatory reading of the primary texts as possible. This approach permits us to see more clearly the two thinkers' similar concerns as well as how (and, to some degree, why) they differed. The point is not to try to find

1. Thorsen, *Calvin vs. Wesley.*

an artificial peace but to enrich the dialogue on a critically important topic and perhaps even further to stimulate new awareness and commitment in the church toward the call to holy living.

The time seems right for a fresh examination. Nearly thirty years ago, Zondervan published *Five Views on Sanctification* in its "Counterpoints" series, which includes representatives of the Wesleyan, Reformed, Pentecostal, Keswick and Dispensationalist traditions. In addition to summarizing their respective positions, each author also contributed a brief critique of the other contributions. In 1996, Zondervan re-released this work without revision and it continues to circulate. While it provides important clarifications, it remains tied to a particular time in the life of American Protestantism. In the second decade of the twenty-first century, while it is true that certain problems are perennial, Christians face new challenges.[2] In what is commonly regarded as a post-Christian America with a changing religious landscape, we find ourselves in need of considering how to offer a unified witness even as we continue to recognize the value of distinctive doctrinal traditions.

In what follows, I will sketch the basic positions of Calvin and Wesley on the nature and scope of sanctification, particularly with regard to what each man considered possible to experience in this life. When talking about this subject, they tended to use divergent scriptural passages, and in explicating those passages, they had different types of adversaries in mind. Even when there is overlap, they apply those scriptures to different types of problems. For example, on the question of the witness of the Spirit, Calvin leaned most heavily on 1 John 5:6–8 while Wesley used Romans 8:15–16. Each was looking for ways to ground Christian confidence but with different frames of reference. The use of Scripture helps us to see the particular concerns each theologian had.

Regarding sources for this study, both Calvin and Wesley wrote expansively and their interpreters have also provided a vast literature. It clearly goes beyond the scope of this contribution to take proper account of such a large body of combined work. The approach herein represents a small *ad fontes* attempt, even while admitting my own implicit and explicit

---

2. A generation of Catholic-Protestant dialogues, especially Catholic-Evangelical ones, has produced new channels of rapprochement. On the other side, the growing religious and moral pluralism in American society has created deep divisions within denominations, creating new tensions. As a result, theologically orthodox Calvinists and Wesleyans may find that they have more in common with each other than they do with some of their denominational fellow travelers.

dependence on interpreters. "Going back to the basics," so to speak, and sticking to primary texts for descriptions of the nature of sanctification offers the possibility of seeing the topic afresh. Therefore, this essay will focus on John Calvin's *Institutes of the Christian Religion* and on a limited number of relevant sermons by Wesley as well as his consummate statement on sanctification, *A Plain Account of Christian Perfection*.

Before turning to specific ideas related to the main question, I offer here what I take from the two thinkers as a similar starting point regarding human nature and the general human condition. Both Calvin and Wesley assumed a body-soul dualism. While Calvin conceptualized the soul as basically of two parts—understanding and will—and Wesley spoke of it in terms of the three dimensions of the image of God—natural, moral, and political—their descriptions tend to follow similar trajectories. Likewise, they both assumed a historical Adam and Eve and a historical Fall. Each had a robust sense of the power of original or inborn sin and its ongoing consequences.

From this common starting point, we find notable divergence: for instance, in the logic of conversion, in what they emphasize regarding the nature of saving faith, regarding which side of the line they place temptation (is it sin or not?), and in what is the extent of sanctification during the believer's earthly life. While many people know well that "Calvinists" and "Wesleyans" disagree on these matters, returning to these thinkers' key writings can aid today's Christians in their understanding and practice.

John Calvin: Sanctification's Limits

John Calvin's life spanned roughly two-thirds of the sixteenth century (1509–1564) and took place in the throes of theological controversy associated with the Protestant Reformation. When he arrived in Geneva, Switzerland in 1536, he had already written the first edition of the *Institutes*. This work was originally written as a manual for new Christians but also as an introduction to Protestant thought for the King of France. It went through at least five editions in Calvin's lifetime and as many as eleven by 1632 and was published both in Latin and French.[3] It became the basis of study in the famous Academy of Geneva and significantly helped to spread Calvin's thought throughout Europe and eventually to America.

---

3. For more background information, see generally Steinmetz, *Calvin in Context*.

The *Institutes* is organized into four books. Book I examines "The Knowledge of God the Creator" (Theology) and Book II considers "The Knowledge of God the Redeemer" (Christology). Notice the emphasis on knowledge given in the titles and carried through the books. Calvin puts heavy emphasis on the mind and on knowledge (*scientia*) while also avoiding dry intellectualism. Interspersed in these sections are long reflections on human fallibility and sin that lead away from proper knowledge of God. Book IV is taken up mainly with ecclesiology.

Of particular interest to me for the present chapter is Book III, "The Way We Receive the Grace of Christ," a section that, more to the point, deals with how Calvin thinks of sanctification, especially Christian perfection.[4] The term "perfection" strikes most Christians as extreme and unrealistic, as it did Calvin. Since Wesley advocates for the doctrine (while using a number of terms interchangeably), it appears on first glance that we should expect fundamental and perhaps even intractable disagreement between these two figures on this particular matter. A consideration of their particular contexts and points of emphases will mollify that impression to some degree.

As mentioned previously, Calvin conceptually divided the soul into two parts, understanding and will, with a hierarchical view of the two. The understanding not only covers cognitive ability (that is, the grasping of concepts)[5] but also the moral sense, which can recognize good and evil. Calvin clarifies these powers of the soul in this way: The understanding "distinguish[es] between objects" while the will "choose[es] and follow[s] what the understanding pronounces good" and rejects what is evil.[6] The understanding, therefore, "is the leader and governor of the soul"[7] over the will.

Through sin, humans have suffered the loss of understanding, wisdom, virtue, holiness, truth, and justice. They can no longer distinguish between objects; they choose and follow what the understanding pronounces good. Reason, though not completely wiped out, is weakened and corrupted.[8] Even "geniuses," the most competent philosophers, "are like a

---

4. It should also be noted that this book includes material on eschatology.

5. For Calvin, the five physical senses are included under the concept "understanding."

6. Calvin, *Institutes of the Christian Religion*, 194.

7. Ibid.

8. See ibid., 270.

traveler passing through a field at night who in a momentary lightning flash sees far and wide, but the sight vanishes so swiftly that he is plunged again into the darkness of the night before he can take even a step."[9] With regard to earthly things, reason still functions, but it is powerless to understand heavenly things.[10] With the loss of sound reason, the will is subject to pride, vainglory, and unbelief. The major point to keep in mind is that, in Calvin's thinking, there is always a moral dimension to knowledge. Sin is not just ignorance; it is delusion.

God's saving grace reverses the consequence of sin so that the understanding can work according to God's creative intention. Here we find one of Calvin's well-known and important distinctions. In the new birth, the will is converted first and then the understanding is transformed:

> Since the Lord in coming to our aid bestows upon us what we lack, when the nature of his work in us appears, our destitution will, on the other hand, at once be manifest. When the apostle tells the Philippians he is confident "that he who began a good work in you will bring it to completion at the day of Jesus Christ" [Phil 1:6], there is no doubt that through "the beginning of a good work" he denotes the very origin of conversion itself, which is in the will. God begins his good work in us . . . by arousing love and desire and zeal for righteousness in our hearts; or, to speak more correctly, by bending, forming, and directing, our hearts to righteousness.[11]

The conversion of the will allows the person to express faith in Christ. Logically, new birth precedes justification by faith.

In Calvin's system, faith is a species of knowledge, keeping in mind that knowledge always has a moral dimension. As the will is transformed, the understanding is able to recognize the nature and purposes of God. Thus, to exercise the faith of a Christian requires constant learning.[12] The Holy Spirit illumines the mind and guides the understanding.[13] To this end Calvin made use of two well-known scriptures, Ephesians 4:23 and Romans 12:2, each referring to the need for the renewal of the mind. The work of the Spirit, over time, chases away ignorance and delusion and restores one to true knowledge of God and to true virtue.

---

9. Ibid., 277.
10. Ibid., 272–77. Calvin references 1 John 1:4–5.
11. Ibid., 297. "Heart" in this quote is synonymous with the will.
12. See ibid., 565.
13. See ibid., 279.

Here we step aside momentarily from the description to note Calvin's context. With whom is he arguing over the nature of saving faith? One finds in this section of the *Institutes* numerous references to the "Schoolmen." Here is but one such criticism: "In this matter the Schoolmen go completely astray, who in considering faith identify it with a bare and simple assent arising out of knowledge, and leave out confidence and assurance of heart."[14] The phrase "arising out of knowledge" helps to show why Calvin emphasized the sequence of conversion, that the will is converted prior to the understanding and then the mind accepts the grace of God offered in Christ, resulting in justification. He regarded the Scholastic view as too naïve regarding the power of sin, particularly with how sin distorts the human ability to know. There is no room in Calvin's view for co-operant grace.

This observation, one of many such in this section, suggests both a similarity to John Wesley's thought but also a difference. Both Calvin and Wesley (after his theological re-orientation in March 1738 and his Aldersgate experience two months later) were concerned to avoid a strictly notional understanding of faith that did not engage the affections and the will. But they also have differing concerns: Calvin wanted to correct a Scholastic view of the extent of human sin and the scope of divine grace while Wesley, influenced by the Pietists, sought to overcome the gap between profession and experience. This difference of concern produces a different view of one of the questions at hand. Since Calvin emphasized faith as a species of knowledge, any doubt (the understanding's temptation to unbelief) that a Christian experiences is expressive of the ongoing presence of sin.

We will return to this point shortly, but before we do, we need to round out this sketch of Calvin's view of sanctification. He uses the word "regeneration" as essentially a synonym for sanctification, and identifies regeneration with repentance: "I interpret repentance as regeneration, whose sole end is to restore in us the image of God that had been disfigured and all but obliterated through Adam's transgression."[15] Here we can see again Calvin's logic, with implications for understanding his caution about the scope of sanctification in this life. As faith (an aspect of the conversion of the understanding) follows logically from the conversion of the will in new birth, so repentance follows faith: "Now it ought to be a fact beyond controversy that repentance not only constantly follows faith, but is also born

---

14. Ibid., 581.
15. Ibid., 601.

of faith."[16] Repentance as a function of sanctification suggests the ongoing need for it. Sin, though no longer dominant, remains.

Repentance involves two movements, mortification of the flesh and vivification by the Spirit. As for mortification, after referencing several Old Testament statements, Calvin turns to Romans 8:7 ("The mind set on the flesh is hostile toward God") and says, "But since all emotions of the flesh are hostility against God, the first step toward obeying his law is to deny our own nature."[17] Vivification refers to the fruits that follow from mortification: righteousness, judgment, and mercy. Demonstration of these qualities "comes to pass when the Spirit of God so imbues our souls, steeped in his holiness, with both new thoughts and feelings, that they can be rightly considered new."[18] Calvin then makes reference to the renewal of our nature according to Ephesians 4:22–23.

This summary of this portion of Calvin's thought helps us to see particularly relevant points for understanding the similarities and differences in his views and John Wesley's. Mortification of the flesh is a process. It continues to recognize the impact of sin as pervasive ignorance of God and of positive hostility toward God. We do not yet know God fully. Sanctification involves the renewing (again we note the continuous action) of our minds whereby we grow in knowledge of God. Any evidence of temptation, therefore, as we shall see momentarily, is evidence of sin remaining, because that temptation signals continuing hostility or ignorance. This reality occupies the believer for the duration of one's earthly life. As Calvin notes,

> And indeed, this restoration does not take place in one moment or one day or one year; but through continual and sometimes even slow advances God wipes out in his elect the corruptions of the flesh, cleanses them of guilt, consecrates them to himself as temples renewing all their minds to true purity that they may practice repentance throughout their lives and know that this warfare will end only at death."[19]

Given this understanding, we can see why Calvin thought of temptation to sin as actually a manifestation of sin and why, therefore, sin is a constant presence until death.

---

16. Ibid., 593.
17. Ibid., 600.
18. Ibid.
19. Ibid., 601.

These considerations lead to the additional question: How does Calvin describe temptation? He remarks that "the saints are as yet so bound by that disease of concupiscence that they cannot withstand being at times tickled and incited either to lust or to avarice or to ambition, or to other vices."[20] Any time we feel a "tickling" or "incitement" toward sin, we must recognize this movement in the soul as evidence of sin itself, because that movement is a manifestation of concupiscence, that is, any disordered desire, born both from the understanding that misreads an evil for a good *and* from the inability of the will to follow the understanding's lead in directing the desire toward its proper end. As Calvin notes,

> We . . . deem it sin when man is tickled by any desire at all against the law of God. Indeed, we label "sin" that very depravity which begets in us desires of this sort. We accordingly teach that in the saints, until they are divested of mortal bodies, there is always sin; for in their flesh there resides that depravity of inordinate desiring which contends against righteousness."[21]

Therefore, all Christians continue to suffer from sin because they undergo temptation. Clearly, Calvin saw temptation as itself sin.

These convictions along with controversies with specific adversaries (particularly Catholics and Anabaptists) predisposed Calvin to dismiss any notion of sinless perfection. His view of faith as a species of knowledge makes him acutely aware of the *mental* strivings associated with doubt and fear and with temptation of any sort. The life of the mind, the thought-life of a person, Calvin argued, provides strong evidence for the continued presence of sin, even in believers.

Therefore, Calvin will have none of the idea of sinless perfection. It is worth returning again momentarily to context and considering how much Calvin's views on this point were shaped by his worry about the claims of the Anabaptists:

> Certain Anabaptists of our day conjure up some sort of frenzied excess instead of spiritual regeneration. The children of God, they assert, *restored to the state of innocence*, now need not take care to bridle the lust of the flesh, but should rather follow the Spirit as their guide, under whose impulsion they can never go astray.[22]

---

20. Ibid., 602.
21. Ibid., 603.
22. Ibid., 606; emphasis added.

This statement comes under the heading "Against the illusion of perfection." Calvin describes these "Anabaptists"[23] as engaging in an extreme and perverse logic, according to which, since we have been delivered from the "curse of old Adam," there will be "no difference between fornication and chastity," as long as one yields to the prompting of the Spirit.[24] We will see momentarily in the case of Wesley that if "perfection" means a return to a pre-Fall state of righteousness, then such perfection is not possible this side of the believer's glorification in heaven. In other words, on the view of perfection set by this context, Wesley would agree with Calvin.

John Wesley: Sanctification's Possibilities

John Wesley's life spanned virtually the entire eighteenth century, from 1703 to 1791. He had no doctrinal quarrel with the Mother (Anglican) Church, while Calvin's task was, in effect, to help establish a newly reformed church on a more scriptural basis. Wesley aimed to reform the nation and to spread "scriptural Christianity" by emphasizing the experiential dimension of evangelical doctrines (sin, repentance, justification, new birth) and by putting into practice scriptural teachings, especially with regard to holiness of heart and life. Given his context, the twin concerns of experience and application prompted Wesley to take a more positive reading of the possibilities of sanctification than the one we found in Calvin.

As I mentioned at the outset, Wesley held to a conventional (for his day) body-soul dualism similar to Calvin's. Furthermore, he also believed that inborn or original sin infected every aspect and fiber of human nature and experience. The natural image of God (the reasoning power) has been deprived of the knowledge of God, though we still have inklings of and hunger for God. Likewise, sin has ruined our ability to recognize and choose the good. Like Calvin, Wesley understands sanctification as progressively overcoming the effects of sin by the renewal of the image of God in the human being.

23. The Münster Rebellion of 1534–1535, led mainly by Melchior Hoffman, was a particularly strong eschatological/apocalyptic movement attempting to establish Münster as the New Jerusalem. Anabaptists in general were perceived during this time as very disruptive of social order.

24. Ibid., 606. Wesley would have put these folks in the category of "enthusiasts" and he, too, did not believe that we could be restored to angelic or Adamic perfection, even though, in the polemics of the eighteenth century, detractors of Wesley and the Methodists tried to pin similar charges on them. See "On Perfection," 72–73.

Also like Calvin, Wesley conceived of the new birth and justification by faith as logically distinguishable. Unlike Calvin, he did not seek to make a strong case for the priority of one over the other. Whereas Calvin, keen to avoid the problems of Scholasticism over the extent of human sin, clearly gives priority to new birth as preceding and making possible justification, Wesley thought of these two movements in terms of a complex whole rather than a sequence. Again we see that context matters. Wesley was worried about other concerns, including bare assent without any actual heart engagement, a problem that seemed to him to dominate in his day. This concern was coupled with his own memory of the lack of salvific confidence he felt earlier in his life, an experience shared by many of his contemporaries.

Therefore, whereas Wesley clearly recognized the knowledge-dimension of faith, unlike Calvin, he tended to speak of faith more in terms of confidence than knowledge. In the sermon placed preeminently at the beginning of Wesley's published sermons, he describes justifying faith in this way: "It is a sure confidence which a man hath in God, that through the merits of Christ *his* sins are forgiven, and *he* reconciled to the favour of God; and in consequence hereof a closing with him and cleaving to him as our 'wisdom, righteousness, sanctification, and redemption' or, in one word, our salvation."[25] He further stresses this connotation of confidence in his sermon, "On Faith," where he expounds and applies Hebrews 11:1. Wesley summarizes the heart of this verse as a "divine evidence and conviction" of things not seen.[26] The Holy Spirit applies this faith—a gift from God—to the believer, resulting in "a childlike confidence in him."[27] Thus, while Calvin examined how the mind is renewed in sanctification, Wesley was concerned that people gain confidence for living the Christian life. Thus, though they cover similar territory, Calvin and Wesley have different purposes.

How did Wesley deal with sin and repentance post-entry into the faith? In the sermon, "On Sin in Believers," we find some assistance in answering this query. The scripture text, 2 Corinthians 5:17, frames Wesley's aim: "Therefore if any man be in Christ, he is a new creature: old things are passed away; behold, all things are become new." This text prompts Wesley to consider how sin remains in believers following justification, for which he provides this definition of sin: "By 'sin,' I here understand inward sin:

25. Wesley, "Salvation by Faith," 121.
26. Wesley, "On Faith," 492.
27. Ibid., 498.

any sinful temper, passion, or affection; such as pride, self-will, love of the world, in any kind or degree; such as lust, anger, peevishness; any disposition contrary to the mind which was in Christ."[28] He concludes that sin does remain, but that, since we are new creations in Christ, sin does not reign.

We notice here Wesley's attention to dispositions or affections or attitudes that, in Wesley's way of thinking, inevitably eventuate into behaviors. While Calvin would agree, what we do not see in Wesley's list are concerns about ignorance or the mind's hostility toward God. Wesley would in like manner agree that the challenges Calvin addresses are worthy of attention. He simply has another set of problems in mind.

In fact, in a number of places in this sermon, Wesley's views sound quite similar to Calvin's. Near the beginning, for example, Wesley, following the Anglican Articles of Religion, defines original sin as "the corruption of the nature of every man . . . whereby man is . . . in his own nature inclined to evil, so that the flesh lusteth contrary to the Spirit."[29] However, he immediately proceeds to what he considers two extremes. Some of the Reformed churches of his day "seem to carry the thing too far . . . as scare to allow that [the believer] has any dominion over [sin], but rather is in bondage thereto."[30] On the other extreme are the Moravians under Count Zinzendorf's direction who, according to Wesley, argued that even the *being* of sin is removed, so that sin no longer even remains, "that even the corruption of nature *is no more* in those who believe in Christ."[31]

Likewise, in his sermon, "The Repentance of Believers," Wesley acknowledges the tenacity of sin that Calvin noted:

> Indeed [the presence of sin] is so evident a truth that wellnigh all the children of God, scattered abroad, however they differ in other points, yet generally agree in this, that although we may "by the Spirit, mortify the deeds of the body," resist and conquer both outward and inward sin, although we may *weaken* our enemies day by day, yet we cannot *drive them out*. By all the grace which is given at justification we cannot extirpate them. Though we watch and pray ever so much, we cannot wholly cleanse either our hearts or hands.[32]

28. Wesley, "On Sin in Believers," 320.
29. Ibid., 318.
30. Ibid.
31. Ibid., 319.
32. Ibid., 346.

Even more plainly, Wesley admits elsewhere that many Christians understand sin in the way Calvin described it. Even every mistake:

> is a transgression of the perfect law . . . Every such mistake, were it not for the blood of atonement, would expose to eternal damnation . . . It follows, that the most perfect have continual need of the merits of Christ, even for their actual transgressions, and may say for themselves, as well as for their brethren, "Forgive us our trespasses." This easily accounts for what might otherwise seem to be utterly unaccountable; namely, that those who are not offended when we speak of the highest degree of love, yet will not hear of living without sin. The reason is, they know all men are liable to mistake, and that in practice as well as in judgment. But they do not know, or do not observe, that this is not sin, if love is the sole principle of action.[33]

Yet, while agreeing with this broader understanding of sin, the latter part of Wesley's statement suggests the trajectory we will need to follow to understand his differences from Calvin. Yes, generally, we could agree that every mistake, every slip of the tongue, every expression of an infirmity reflects the fallenness of human nature and thus the continuing tenacity of sin even for believers. But Wesley wanted to know, What do we make of all the scriptures that speak to transformation? For this reason he explained sin in a sort of macro and micro way—sin broadly conceived (as Calvin does) and sin "properly so-called" where the main attention goes to the willfulness of sin, the conscious and direct affront to God's holiness.

On this point, Wesley considers how best to understand important scriptures found in 1 John 2 and 3, where we find references to "conquering the evil one" and to those who commit sin being children of the devil rather than children of God. Wesley was trying to make sense of such scriptures in light of the work of Christ and with regard to sin post-conversion. These efforts helped to shape his understanding of temptation and his optimism for Christian perfection or full sanctification.

Taking this narrower view of sin, Wesley thus did not consider temptation as sin. In his sermon "On Temptation," the scripture verse theme is 1 Corinthians 10:13,[34] which serves as both a warning and a promise. It warns

---

33. Wesley, *A Plain Account of Christian Perfection*, 52–53.

34. The Authorized Version reads, "There hath no temptation taken you but such as is common to man. And God is faithful, who will not suffer you to be tempted above that ye are able; but will with the temptation also make a way to escape, that ye may be able to bear it."

people not to become presumptuously self-sufficient about their ability to succeed in the Christian life, and it promises that, with every temptation, the Lord provides a way of escape. Since we all suffer temptation, Wesley seeks to encourage his readers by considering the myriad sources of temptation. He works through a series of easily recognizable situations and conditions: our own weaknesses and disorders of body and soul, the disordered condition of the world at large, and even the infirmities and jarring quirks of people who are otherwise exemplary Christians. He extends this picture to include temptations caused by the principalities and powers in spiritual realms.[35] Considering the nature of the fallen world, believers face many temptations to sin, but temptation—understood as Wesley does—is not to be identified or lumped in with the affections and dispositions that clearly reveal a heart not yet yielded to Christ. To say it a slightly different way and to put words in Wesley's mouth: we need not repent of temptation, but we do need to repent of sin. Furthermore, repentance as a humble attitude of appropriate self-awareness sensitizes believers to the need for watching and praying so that one does not fall into sin.

Repentance as an attitude or disposition thus plays a different role for Wesley than for Calvin. A survey of the sermon "The Repentance of Believers" shows Wesley's interest in dispositions and affections and the need for awareness of how the heart wrongly attaches to objects other than the one true God. To this end, Wesley distinguishes two dimensions of repentance that Calvin does not:

> And this is undoubtedly true, that there is a repentance and a faith which are more especially necessary at the beginning: a repentance which is a conviction of our utter sinfulness and guiltiness and helplessness, and which precedes our receiving that kingdom of God which our Lord observes "is within us" . . . But notwithstanding this, there is also a repentance and a faith . . . which are requisite after we have "believed the gospel"; yea, and in every subsequent stage of our Christian course . . . And this repentance and faith are full as necessary, in order to our continuance and growth in grace, as the former faith and repentance were in order to our entering into the kingdom of God.[36]

---

35. See Wesley, "On Temptation," 159–62. Wesley sounds particularly "modern" in this section of his sermon as he recognizes the link between physical debilities and spiritual discouragement of the sort that tempts one to sin.

36. Wesley, "The Repentance of Believers," 335–36.

Repentance for Wesley, therefore, is primarily a form of self-knowledge rather than of mortification and vivification. It is as much an attitude as a practice. The Christian must remain aware of the ongoing challenges associated with pride, self-will and unbelief—the sources of the sin that remains, even if it does not reign.

We see here Wesley's attempt at nuance, his trying to take account of a broad range of concerns and scriptures. For example, how do we understand the claims in First John 2 and 3 that Christians do not sin? How do we make sense of the new birth, of regeneration, and of the new creation if we continue to sin? What do we make of Paul's rhetorical question in Romans 6, "Shall we continue in sin that grace may abound?" Wesley's efforts in this regard point us back to context. On one side, like Calvin, Wesley seeks to correct the problem of works-righteousness found in his day. A complication that goes beyond the scope of this study involves differences surrounding understandings of "works-righteousness" between Calvin's and Wesley's days. Wesley faced a "do the best you can" morality associated with formality in religious observance and with deism. In this sense, our time is more like Wesley's than Calvin's. Furthermore, Wesley battled antinomian tendencies among the Moravians, with whom he began his evangelical journey, whereas Calvin opposed the antinomian tendencies of the Anabaptists. We can recognize general similarities in these matters, but we would still need to look at more fine-grained distinctions. They would help us understand more clearly the differences between these two church figures.

We come now to the linchpin of Wesley's theology: the doctrine of Christian perfection. The aim of the Christian life is full sanctification. At a surface level, it appears that we could find no more clear-cut or entrenched division between Calvinists and Wesleyans than this theme. In the sermon "Christian Perfection," Wesley admits the paradoxical impossibility yet necessity of aiming at what "Christian perfection" entails, but he also reveals his belief that the doctrine is thoroughly scriptural:

> There is scarce any expression in Holy Writ which has given more offence than this. The word "perfect" is what many cannot bear. The very sound of it is an abomination to them . . . And hence some have advised, wholly to lay aside the use of those expressions, "because they have given so great offence." But are they not found

in the oracles of God? If so, by what authority can any messenger of God lay them aside, even though all men should be offended?[37]

In the rhetorical question that ends this quote, we can see the responsibility Wesley felt to get this doctrine as "right" as possible. In fact, Wesley was convinced that God had called the Methodists into existence (and placed him as their leader) to promulgate this doctrine and to embody it in their practices.[38] The doctrine speaks to the quality of life to which Christian believers, according to Wesley, are to aspire and to believe. This quality of life is by God's grace and is for this life and not simply for the next.

To make his case, Wesley had to speak both to what he did *not* mean as well as what he did mean by the term. Even in being made perfect in love, one could not expect to gain freedom from ignorance and from infirmities or mistakes. Most assuredly, one could not expect ever to be free of temptation, which gives us a glimpse at why Wesley did not consider temptation as sin *per se*. One could, on the other hand, look to God for the gift of full sanctification (understood as a gift of God's grace on par with the gift of justification), as this aim served as the motive for continuing to grow in the grace and knowledge of the Lord.[39]

How, then, did Wesley describe Christian perfection? One of his most succinct descriptions (and there are many) comes from the sermon "On Perfection," with Hebrews 6:1 as the text: "Therefore leaving the principles of the doctrine of Christ, let us go on unto perfection; not laying again the foundation of repentance from dead works, and of faith toward God" (Authorized Version). While we are still in the body, the Christian can reasonably expect God to grant the following set of dispositions, with their concomitant actions:

> It is the "loving the Lord his God with all his heart, and with all his soul, and with all his mind." This is the sum of Christian perfection: it is all comprised in that one word, love. The first branch of

---

37. Wesley, "Christian Perfection," 99–100.

38. As already quoted in this volume, Wesley remarks in a "Letter to Robert Carr Brackenbury, 15 September 1790" that "this doctrine is the grand depositum which God has lodged with the people called Methodists" (238).

39. Wesley also took great care in making sure people did not use "infirmities" as an excuse for moral laxity. In the sermon "Christian Perfection," he warns, "Only let us take care to understand this word aright. Let us not give that soft title to known sins, as the manner of some is" (103). After listing a group of such "infirmities" as drunkenness and returning "railing for railing," Wesley states, "It is plain that all you who thus speak, if ye repent not, shall with your infirmities go quick into hell" (103).

it is the love of God: and as he that loves God loves his brother also, it is inseparably connected with the second, "Thou shalt love thy neighbour as thyself." Thou shalt love every man as thy own soul, as Christ loved us. "On these two commandments hang all the law and the prophets": these contain the whole of Christian perfection.[40]

In a number of places, Wesley speaks about this same love from a variety of angles: having the mind of Christ and walking as he walked (Phil 2:5–11), exhibiting the fruit of the Spirit (Gal 5:22–23), being renewed in the image of God (Eph 4 and Col 3), being "holy in all manner of conversation" (1 Pet 1:15), and being sanctified entirely (1 Thess 5:23).

Nonetheless, Wesley faced probably more controversy about this teaching than any other he sought to advance. *A Plain Account of Christian Perfection* collected and summarized Wesley's thoughts and teachings from 1725 up to the point of its publication in 1777. This treatise includes references to the *Minutes* of Methodist conferences, discussions of scriptural passages such as the ones mentioned above, excerpts from Charles Wesley's hymns, and even testimonies of full sanctification from people in the Methodist movement. It summarizes points I have made above with reference to various sermons.

In short, Wesley taught that, by God's grace, a believer could truly experience singleness of intention: to love God without reserve and to love one's neighbor as oneself. Likewise with regard to intention, God's grace can free the believer from pride and self-will, and God can grant this gift to a believer in this life. In its barest essence, then, Christian perfection entails the work of the Holy Spirit in the transformation of dispositions, affections, and tempers so that believers demonstrate Christ's character and serve Christ's purposes. It does not mean perfection of performance or freedom from the afflictions and limitations of living in a fallen world.

Conclusion

This brief summary of the Swiss reformer and the Anglican divine regarding sanctification reveals shades of meaning and points of emphasis that help us see how their thoughts converge and diverge. Both uphold an evangelical faith that supersedes bare intellectual assent. Both men portray high sensitivity for God's holiness and for utter devotion to Christ. Each refuses

---

40. Wesley, "On Perfection," 74.

to take the easy way with regard to the challenges of Christian commitment. In that vein, each man takes the problem of sin with utmost seriousness, and the need for ongoing repentance and holy living is highlighted by both. Calvin and Wesley recognize the power of the inclinations of the heart in sin and in sanctification, once the Spirit of God has gotten hold of a person. Significantly, Calvin places temptation on one side of the line relative to sin and Wesley on the other. This difference leads Calvin toward a degree of pessimism in imagining what is possible for the Christian in this life, while for Wesley it evoked optimism. Where Calvin saw limits, Wesley saw possibilities.

Therefore, our exploration illustrates both the frustration of theological controversy and the possibilities for productive ecumenical dialogue. To use a hackneyed sports cliché, I find the core ideas of Calvin and Wesley regarding sanctification to be "in the ballpark" of each other. At the same time, it is worth considering that, in a significant way, they are not really talking about the same thing. If this observation holds true, it means that there is good reason to return to both men's ideas, laying them systematically side by side, taking full account of the theological controversies in which each was embroiled, and seeing if we cannot resolve some of the differences that still bedevil their doctrinal heirs.

8

John Wesley and John Paul II on the Eucharist and Holiness

Stephen Sours

For as often as you eat this bread and drink the cup, you proclaim the Lord's death until he comes

(1 Cor 11:26, NRSV)

IN THE CELEBRATION OF the Eucharist, the church fully shares in the reconciling work of the cross. What Jesus accomplished in his death and resurrection he gives to the church, and the church in union with its Savior gives it back to God the Father. This event is at once an ecclesial and individual participation in the body and blood of Christ. For both John Wesley and John Paul II, the soteriological dimension of the sacrament lies at the heart of their eucharistic theology. "The Church draws her life from the Eucharist," the pope joyfully declares at the beginning of *Ecclesia de Eucharistia*;[1] likewise for Wesley, Christians receive nothing short of the "the full salvation which God has promised to his people."[2] This partici-

---

1. John Paul II, *EE*, 1.
2. Wesley, *CSS*, 4.

pation in Christ—died, raised, and glorified—through the Spirit, which is the church's sacrificial worship to the Father, is the source and summit of holiness in the Christian life.

The pairing of John Paul II and John Wesley as dialogue partners on the Eucharist and holiness might not spring readily to mind. What, theologically speaking, do a Vatican II-era pontiff and an eighteenth-century Anglican priest (and a revivalist outlier at that) have in common? Are they not, each in his own way, fathers of communities that have suffered from deep mistrust and division, and which, despite decades of reconciliation and fruitful dialogue, remain separated around the communion table? David Chapman notes that Wesley's dealings with Roman Catholicism were both critical and complex, as the juxtaposition between the irenic "Letter to a Roman Catholic" and the critical "Popery Calmly Considered" clearly demonstrates.[3]

If we keep our gaze on Wesley and the pope a little longer, however, a much richer picture comes into focus: for these two pastors, the Eucharist is the principal cause of holiness in the Christian life. To be sure, while John Paul II's *Ecclesia de Eucharistia* and John Wesley's *Christian Sacrament and Sacrifice* and *Hymns on the Lord's Supper* are key traditioning texts in their respective traditions, they are also quite different texts—written for different purposes and different audiences—that are not in full doctrinal agreement; nevertheless, at the heart of each lies a common, joyful, soteriological proclamation: by sharing in the body and blood of Christ, Christians are forgiven, sanctified, transformed, and empowered to lead lives of holiness in imitation of Christ. This chapter affords the opportunity to celebrate this common eucharistic proclamation.

The pope's treatise is clearly much broader than Wesley's, touching on the issues of ecclesiology, the hierarchical priesthood, ecumenism, and eucharistic practice. Yet their common soteriology is found in the pope's first chapter and throughout Wesley's text. In chapter one, the pope reflects on the saving work of Christ in the Eucharist and organizes his teaching around the words of the *mysterium fidei*: *Christ has died, Christ is risen, Christ will come again*. Indeed, in many respects, Wesley's entire text is

---

3. Chapman, *In Search of the Catholic Spirit*; see his opening chapter, "John Wesley and Roman Catholicism" (6–43). On the one hand, while Wesley's anti-Catholic sentiments likely strike contemporary Methodists as abrasive and even embarrassing, his rhetoric was typical of the Anglicanism of his day. On the other hand—and at his best—Wesley managed to rise above the polemics of his context and cast a vision of a catholic spirit that far anticipated the ecumenical movement.

an extended reflection on this eucharistic acclamation.[4] Both Wesley and the pope follow a loose chronological progression beginning with Christ's institution of the Supper and sacrificial death on to the church's sacrificial discipleship and eschatological hope. Threaded all the way through this progression in each of these texts is the saving work of Christ in the Eucharist and its effect, Christian holiness. By holiness is meant the gracious process of becoming ever more a friend of God. As Wesley puts it: "Gospel holiness is no less than the image of God stamped upon the heart. It is no other than the whole mind which was in Christ Jesus."[5]

Christ Has Died

John Paul and John Wesley are careful to demonstrate how the Eucharist is a participation in God's salvation history, and they both insist that the locus of this saving work is the death and resurrection of Jesus. The holiest days of Jesus' life and ministry—the Triduum—are the focus of both the church's soteriological reflection and its sacramental worship: "those days embrace the *mysterium paschale*; they also embrace the *mysterium eucharisticum*."[6] The pope continues, "At every celebration of the Eucharist, we are spiritually brought back to the paschal Triduum: to the events of the evening of Holy Thursday, to the Last Supper and to what followed it."[7] The *mysterium fidei* is the church's assent and proclamation of the *mysterium paschale* in the midst of its celebration of the *mysterium eucharisticum*: "Her foundation and wellspring is the whole *Triduum paschale*, but this is as it were gathered up, foreshadowed and 'concentrated' forever in the gift of the Eucharist."[8]

---

4. Wainwright notes this shared hermeneutic between the pope and John Wesley, and he finds the same ordering in Aquinas's eucharistic theology, where the sacrament functions as a *signum rememorativum, signum demonstrativum,* and *signum prognosticum* (*ST* 3.60.3 [4:2340–41]); see his "Introduction," viii. Looney, too, notes that the central relationship between Christ's presence and Christ's actions in the Eucharist has important ecumenical implications; see "Ecumenical 'Lights' and 'Shadows,'" 105.

5. Wesley, "The New Birth," 194. Quite possibly, every aspect of Christian theology could be poured into eucharistic theology, but that obviously does not mean that every text on the Eucharist can address every doctrine. Neither the pope nor Wesley gives an account of his atonement theology or (what Wesley called) the way of salvation in these texts; nonetheless, these doctrines are latent therein.

6. John Paul II, *EE*, 2.

7. Ibid., 3.

8. Ibid., 5.

The crucifixion of Jesus is the central divine action of justice, mercy, and love on behalf of humankind. While the pope and Wesley do not develop a doctrine of atonement in their texts, they do assert that the atoning work of the Eucharist derives entirely from Jesus' work on the cross. Indeed, in order for the faithful to understand properly what the Eucharist signifies and the grace it conveys, they must understand what Christ accomplished on the cross. Wesley picks up the prominent New Testament images of sacrifice, propitiation, and priesthood from John, Romans, and Hebrews in asserting Christ's death on our behalf in its full trinitarian scope. "The sacrifice of Christ," he writes, "being appointed by the Father for a propitiation that should continue to all ages; and withal being everlasting by the privilege of its own order, which is an unchangeable priesthood, and by his worth who offered it, that is, the blessed Son of God, and by the power of the Eternal Spirit . . . [must] stand eternal, the same yesterday, today, and forever."[9]

For John Paul, a proper eucharistic theology is reliant upon a fitting understanding of Christ's crucifixion; however, such an understanding of the cross is reliant upon Jesus' own interpretation of his death, which he gives to his disciples when he institutes—and in turn interprets—his last supper, the first Lord's Supper. Jesus did not merely state that he was giving his body and blood to his disciples through the eucharistic elements; instead, his explanation of his actions at the supper is also an elaboration of his sacrificial and salvific actions on the cross. Jesus' body was "given for [his disciples]," and his blood was "poured out" for them. Jesus did not just give of himself, "he also expressed its sacrificial meaning and made sacramentally present his sacrifice which would soon be offered on the Cross, for the salvation of all."[10] Recognition of the sacrificial dimension of the

---

9. Wesley, CSS, 6–7. This is not to suggest that Wesley's atonement theology is limited to sacrificial imagery, although he emphasizes it here; he is well-known for incorporating other atoning motifs into his theology, such as Christ's healing, redeeming, and divinizing work. See the range of atonement language, for example, in "Hymn 31" and "Hymn 87" (*HLS*, 24–25 and 74–75, respectively), including "salvation," "rest," "cooling shadow," "redemption," "washing," "pardon," "sanctification," "purity," "release," "apply the blood," "relieve," "cleansing," and "casting."

10. John Paul II, *EE*, 12. Steck offers an interesting reading of sacrifice from the perspective of Christian ethics. He insists that a proper "agential distance" be maintained between God (who initiates and gives) and people who give/sacrifice in response, and in doing so advances an anthropology akin to what Methodists recognize as responsible grace. Christ suffers sacrificially in order to manifest divine love and redress the sin and suffering that humanity causes in this world; consequently, Christian discipleship entails

Eucharist—a cornerstone in Catholic eucharistic theology—is grounded in Jesus' passion, which is a universal, atoning sacrifice given to the church: "this sacrifice is so decisive for the salvation of the human race that Jesus Christ offered it and returned to the Father only after he had left us a means of sharing in it as if we had been present there."[11]

As Wesley interprets the event, the disciples are made to share in Christ's death through the Last Supper in the same manner that Jesus' followers share in Christ today through the Lord's Supper: "He was pleased at his last supper to ordain this, as a holy memorial and representation of what he was then about to suffer." Wesley also sees in the Eucharist the "bread broken" and "wine poured out" as a "partaking" in Christ, that is, as a sacrificial and atoning interpretation of and participation in the cross: "This holy mystery might set forth both the martyrdom and the sacrifice of this crucified saviour; giving up his flesh, shedding his blood, and pouring out his very soul, to atone for their sins."[12] As a memorial of the cross, the Eucharist thus owes its meaning and significance to the meaning and significance of Jesus' sacrificial death.

Sacrament and Sacrifice

John Paul and John Wesley address the sacramental and sacrificial aspects of the Eucharist within the perspective of eucharistic memorial. The anamnetic nature of the Eucharist is a participation in the body and blood of Christ because—as Wesley and the pope insist in no uncertain terms—the Eucharist is much more than a mere memorial of Christ's death. The Eucharist, for them, is an atoning sacrament: it is a sacrament because it participates as an instrument of divine grace, and it is atoning due to the aspect of grace in which it participates, namely the cross. Wesley affirms, "The main intention of Christ herein was not the bare remembrance of his passion; but over and above, to invite us to his sacrifice, not as done and

---

imitating Christ by taking suffering "into the sign of the cross by making it into a moment of self-sacrificial love." He also suggests that the pope's emphasis on Eucharist as sacrifice over a communal banquet fosters the proper agential distance by provoking in us a response of "active love," contemplation, and worship in "muted awe." See "In Union with the Paschal Mystery," 314–19. Relatedly, *HLS* seeks to provoke much the same response by calling worshippers sacramentally back to the cross in contemplation of Christ's suffering and love.

11. John Paul II, *EE*, 11.
12. Wesley, CSS, 5.

gone many years since, but as to grace and mercy, still lasting, still new, still the same as when it was first offered for us."[13] The pope's language illustrates a shared conceptual framework: "In this gift Jesus Christ entrusted to his Church the perennial making present of the paschal mystery. With it he brought about a mysterious 'oneness in time' between that *Triduum* and the passage of the centuries."[14]

As a sacrament, the Eucharist (the rites, the elements, and the people) receives from God a metaphysical reality which is the source of its sharing in divine transcendence. Neither author offers a doctrine of God as part of these eucharistic texts, but their convictions about divine transcendence and immanence permeate their language about the eucharistic memorial as sacrament and sacrifice. John Paul II speaks of a "sacramental re-presentation" of the cross and of "the sacrifice of the Cross perpetuated down the ages."[15] In the Eucharist, the "central event of salvation becomes really present."[16] The church "draws her life from [Christ's] redeeming sacrifice," not just by remembrance but "through a real contact, since this sacrifice is made present ever anew, sacramentally perpetuated"; the Eucharist "applies" to believers in "every age" the "reconciliation won once for all by Christ."[17]

Wesley also operates from a classical conviction of God's "eternal now,"[18] that is, of God's temporal transcendence. He, too, speaks of the Eucharist as a "representation," of making the cross "really present for us as if it were newly done." The eucharistic elements "expose . . . His sufferings, as if they were present now." On the altar, Wesley sees that which is "somewhat very like the sacrifice of my saviour." To worship at the Lord's Table is akin to being at "the very foot of His Cross."[19] Wesley makes explicit the connection between divine transcendence, Christology, and the sacrament; moreover, his Christology draws from texts such as Romans 8, Hebrews, and Revelation, where Jesus is at once mediator, intercessor, High Priest, victim, and lamb. He remarks,

---

13. Ibid., 6.
14. John Paul II, *EE*, 5.
15. Ibid., 11.
16. Ibid.
17. Ibid., 12
18. This is Borgen's helpful phrase in *John Wesley on the Sacraments*, 45.
19. See Wesley, CSS, 4–7.

> This great and holy mystery communicates to us the death of our Blessed Lord, both as offering himself to God, and as giving himself to man. As he offered himself to God, it enters me into that mystical body for which he died, and which is dead with Christ: yea, it sets me on the very shoulders of that eternal priest, while he offers up himself and intercedes for his spiritual Israel. And by this means it conveys to me the communion of his sufferings, which leads to a communion in all his graces and glories. As he offers himself to man, the holy sacrament is, after the sacrifice for sin, the true sacrifice of peace-offerings, and the table purposely set to receive those mercies that are sent down from his altar.[20]

The Lord's Table, therefore, both "shews" and "offers" the "richest gift a saint can receive," namely, "the Lord Jesus crucified."[21]

The doctrine of eucharistic sacrifice belongs within the theological framework of sacramental memorial, and this is exactly where John Paul II and Wesley discuss it. When a theology of sacrifice is dislodged from a sacramental metaphysics, the interpretation of the church's actions (the minister's and the congregation's) and its use of the eucharistic elements quickly become distorted and misunderstood, which indeed occurred at the Reformation and which has continued between Protestants and Catholics. Despite the theological controversies associated with eucharistic sacrifice, neither Wesley nor the pope evinces any sense of embarrassment or defensiveness about the doctrine because it is such a central—indeed necessary—feature of their eucharistic theologies. In short, because Christ's death was a sacrifice, the meal that applies the holiness of Christ's death must also be a sacrifice. Both theologians are very clear about this reality.

Even while John Paul reaffirms Catholic teaching about eucharistic sacrifice, he does so in a way that is sensitive to a larger ecumenical audience. Jesus' crucifixion for our sake makes his death sacrificial, but his life is first and foremost a sacrifice because it is a self-offering of love and obedience unto the Father. He obediently offers himself to the Father in a life

---

20. Ibid., 15–16. For more on Wesley's sacramental theology, see Staples, *Outward Sign and Inward Grace*. Baptism and Eucharist sometimes have an unsettled role in Methodist practice, since not all Methodists are sacramentalists. The fact that Felton's excellent parish resource *This Holy Mystery* devotes as much time as it does to teaching sacramental theology is illustrative of this tension in United Methodism.

21. Wesley, CSS, 16. Sacramental theology is intimately tied to the doctrine of God, and John Paul and John Wesley unapologetically operate from a classical understanding of God's transcendence, which makes God present at each and every moment in time.

that culminates in a death suffered for all humanity.[22] The cross, therefore, remains the single, unique, and unrepeatable atoning sacrifice of Christ, the holiness of which Christ gives to his church through the sacrament. "The Mass," he writes, "makes present the sacrifice of the Cross; it does not add to that sacrifice nor does it multiply it. What is repeated is its memorial celebration, its 'commemorative representation,' which makes Christ's one, definitive redemptive sacrifice always present in time."[23] Therefore, the Eucharist, as a sacramental representation of the cross, mirrors sacrificially the actions of Christ: "By virtue of its close relationship to the sacrifice of Golgotha, the Eucharist is a sacrifice in the strict sense, and not only in a general way, as if it were simply a matter of Christ's offering himself to the faithful as their spiritual food."[24] At the Last Supper and at every subsequent Eucharist, Christ offers himself primarily to the Father on behalf of humankind because that was the modality of his self-offering on the cross ("my body, which is given [to the Father] for you"). This, then, is the modality of sacrifice in the Eucharist with Christ as the true priest of the sacrament: "In giving his sacrifice to the Church, Christ has also made his own the spiritual sacrifice of the Church, which is called to offer herself in union with the sacrifice of Christ."[25] A sacrament should faithfully represent the reality that it seeks to apply, and the sacramental sacrifice of Christ's body and blood—concentrated on the priest as the minister of Christ—seeks to represent Christ's offering to the Father and to apply his saving grace to the church.

Wesley's teaching on eucharistic sacrifice shares some remarkable conceptual and doctrinal similarities with John Paul II. Section VI of *The Christian Sacrament and Sacrifice* casts the Eucharist as a "Commemorative Sacrifice." Wesley begins with a very strong affirmation, referring both to Christ's death and to the sacrament: "There never was on earth a true religion without some kind of sacrifices." The sacrifices of the Old Testament could neither take away sin (apart from Christ) nor fully represent true worship; however, "Holy Communion alone brings together these two great ends, atonement of sins, and acceptable duty to God."[26] To be

22. See generally John Paul II, *EE*, 13.
23. Ibid., 12.
24. Ibid., 13.
25. Ibid. For a major treatment on these doctrines by a Catholic authority, see Journet, *The Mass*.
26. Wesley, CSS, 20–21.

sure, the atoning power of the sacrament derives exclusively from Christ's all-sufficient and unique sacrifice: "Nevertheless, this sacrifice, which by a real oblation was not to be offered more than once, is, by a devout and thankful commemoration, to be offered up every day."[27]

Wesley's thoughts further align with the pope's with respect to the One to whom the sacrifice is offered, namely the Father, and with respect to how the sacrament mirrors the self-offering of Christ: It is this sacrament "whereby we present before God the Father that precious oblation of his Son once offered. And thus do we every day offer unto God the meritorious sufferings of our Lord." No other form of worship participates in ("reaches") the cross and places "it solemnly forth before the eyes of God" as the Holy Communion does.[28]

Yet another area of convergence between John Wesley and John Paul II is the action of the minister (and the people) at the Altar-Table. At this point, the actions of feasting, receiving, repenting, offering, and forgiving mutually inform one another, as they did at the Last Supper. Moreover, the sacrifice on the cross (represented in the sacrament by the minister, the elements, and the people) is realized by the presence of Christ himself, who is at once the sacrificial Lamb and the High Priest who, in offering himself, intercedes before the Father on behalf of his people.

> To men it is a sacred table where God's minister is ordered to represent from God his master, the passion of his dear Son, as still fresh, and still powerful for their eternal salvation. And to God is an altar whereon men mystically present to him the same sacrifice as still bleeding and suing for mercy. And because it is the High Priest himself, the true anointed of the Lord, who hath set up both this table and the altar, for the communication of his body and blood to men, and for the representation of both to God; it cannot be doubted but that the one is most profitable to the penitent sinner, and the other most acceptable to his gracious Father.[29]

Notice that no disagreement obtains between Wesley and the pope regarding the theology 1) of sacrifice as a sacramental commemorative

27. Ibid., 21.

28. Ibid., 21–22. See also "Hymn 124": "Yet may we celebrate below / and daily thus thine offering show / exposed before thy Father's eyes; / In this tremendous mystery / present thee bleeding on the tree / our everlasting sacrifice" (*HLS*, 105) and "Hymn 122": "Father, let the sinner go / the Lamb did once atone / lo! we to thy justice show / the Passion of thy Son" (*HLS*, 103).

29. Wesley, CSS, 22.

representation and 2) of Christ who offers himself in the sacrament as one who is eternally offering his historically unique sacrifice. Instead, the divergence lies in the teachings on transubstantiation and holy orders. For the pope, Jesus offered himself sacramentally to the Father at the Last Supper, and so the priest does the same in the Eucharist. For Wesley, Jesus' actions at the Supper represented his self-offering, and the people offer it commemoratively to the Father in the Eucharist. Concerning Jesus' actions, Wesley writes that he is "our eternal high priest, who is gone up into the true sanctuary, and doth there continually present both his own body and blood before God," while the church below presents to God the memorial of Jesus' body and blood as a "figure of his sacrifice."[30]

While the differences associated with sacrifice are not insignificant, Wesleyans need not regard uniformity on this matter as an essential (and therefore as an impediment) to unity. Wesley's catholic spirit is much broader by far. More essential is the soteriological reality at the heart of the Eucharist. Both Wesley and John Paul teach that Jesus, through his ministry as High Priest, conveys to the church the atoning grace—the holiness—of his earthly sacrifice, which in the power of the Holy Spirit the church concomitantly offers to the Father in union with her Lord.

Christ Is Risen

The pardon that Christ won on the cross is by no means the end of his sacrifice. The cross is only midway through the Triduum—midway through the *mysterium paschale*—and therefore midway through the *mysterium fidei*. The Eucharist also applies all benefits of Christ's passion to his people. Both authors use the biblical imagery of Jesus as Passover and the Bread of Life, and they also raise the doctrine of his real presence in the sacrament. Moreover, while pneumatology plays a muted role in both treatises, the role of the epiclesis and the gift of the Holy Spirit are emphasized here.

While the offering of the eucharistic elements most closely represents Jesus' death, nevertheless the full scope of his passion is conveyed in the rite. "The eucharistic Sacrifice makes present not only the mystery of the Saviour's passion and death, but also the mystery of the resurrection which crowned his sacrifice," the pope writes; only as the "living and risen One"

---

30. Ibid. For a detailed discussion on this topic, see Sours, "Eucharist and Anthropology"; for an excellent overview of Wesley's theology of sacrifice, see Khoo, *Wesleyan eucharistic Spirituality*, 73–89.

does he become the "bread of life."[31] All the work of Jesus' passion, and not just his atonement, applies to those who receive him in faith.

Jesus is really, substantially, and sacramentally present in the Eucharist in the same manner that he was present in the eucharistic elements at the Last Supper. Jesus' physical absence in subsequent Eucharists in no way distracts from his presence in the host and the chalice. Without offering a long *apologia*—in this context none is needed—John Paul II upholds the church's dogmatic teaching on transubstantiation. He references Aquinas, the Council of Trent, Paul VI, and the charism of the Magisterium in reaffirming the real and substantial presence of Christ in the elements. Contrary to our typical senses and beyond what "human reason fully experiences," a theological account of the eucharistic mystery "must firmly maintain that in objective reality, independently of our mind, the bread and wine have ceased to exist after the consecration."[32] For this reason, then, the adoration of the blessed sacrament is not only a praiseworthy practice but also an "inexhaustible source of holiness."[33]

The real presence of the resurrected Jesus in the Eucharist is the cause of transformation and holiness in the believer, for what the Eucharist communicates specifically is not simply the grace of Jesus' reconciliation (as if that were an insignificant matter), but the presence of the risen Lord himself. This is a joyful event: indeed, it is the highest gift a believer could receive, and it occurs when the believer receives Jesus interiorly. John Paul writes, "The saving efficacy of the sacrifice is fully realized when the Lord's body and blood are received in communion. The eucharistic sacrifice is intrinsically directed to the inward union of the faithful with Christ through communion; we receive the very One who offered himself for us."[34] The pope ties this with Jesus' "bread of life" discourse, which entails a trinitarian dynamic into which Christians are incorporated. Insofar as Jesus "lives because of the Father," so the one who "eats [of him] will live" (John 6:57). As the pope remarks, "the Eucharist is a true banquet, in which Christ offers himself as our nourishment."[35]

31. John Paul II, *EE*, 14.

32. Ibid., 15. Walsh places the pope's teaching on Jesus' real presence in historical context by tracing the development of Catholic thought concerning Jesus' presence in the Eucharist; see "The Presence of the Mystery of Christ in the Broken Bread."

33. John Paul II, *EE*, 10.

34. Ibid., 16.

35. Ibid. Le Bruyns rightly notes that Protestants balk at the doctrine of transubstantiation, but he over-generalizes when he notes that they also stumble over the idea that

This trinitarian dynamic expressly includes the gift of the Holy Spirit. The pope hints at the mutual indwelling of the divine persons when he describes this gift. The Holy Spirit is the one given to the church by Christ and the one who gives to us every other gift. "Through our communion in his body and blood, Christ also grants us his Spirit . . . The Church implores this divine Gift, the source of every other gift, in the eucharistic epiclesis . . . Thus by the gift of his body and blood Christ increases within us the gift of his Spirit."[36]

Wesley also emphasizes nearly identical themes in Sections III and IV of *The Christian Sacrament and Sacrifice*. He, too, celebrates that the Eucharist represents not only the forgiveness which is a result of Christ's sufferings, but likewise the continual spiritual sustenance and holiness of his Passion. A life of holiness requires ongoing spiritual food beyond the initial gift of forgiveness: "Therefore the sacrifice of Christ procures also grace to renew and preserve the life he hath given."[37] The salvation of Christ, once accomplished on the cross, must continually be made a reality in the lives of his people. As the true Passover, he continually feeds from heaven with his body and blood; he creates in the believer a new heart and acts to save and preserve. The symbolism depicted in the sacrament represents not only Christ but what Christ does in the believer. Wesley suggests a strong note of communion and imitation in his prayer: "O Thou who are the truth of what Thou biddest me take, perform in me what Thou dost show. Give me eternal life by those thy sufferings; for here is the body broken: Give also strength and nourishment for this life; for here is the bread of heaven."[38]

Christ is present *"par excellence"* in the Eucharist, for this is precisely what Wesley affirms in "Hymn 91": "If chiefly here thou may'st be found / if now, e'en now we find thee here / O let their joys like ours abound / Invite them to the royal cheer / Feed with imperishable food / And fill their raptured souls with God" (*HLS*, 78); see *"Ecclesia de Eucharistia*: On its Ecumenical Import," 122.

36. John Paul II, *EE*, 17. Methodists will hear in these words the epiclesis from their Great Thanksgiving, except that in their eucharistic prayer it is the Father who is asked to "pour out your Holy Spirit on us gathered here, and on these gifts of bread and wine."

37. Wesley, CSS, 10.

38. Ibid., 12. *Hymns on the Lord's Supper* is ripe with allusions to food, feasting, banquets, and the like. Consider "Hymn 84" in which Jesus is both the host and the meal, imagery with which the pope would agree: "Jesus, master of the feast / the feast itself Thou art / now receive thy meanest guest/ and comfort every heart: / Give us living bread to eat / Manna that from heaven comes down / fill us with immortal meat / and make thy nature known" (*HLS*, 72).

Spiritual sustenance and nourishment are indeed wonderful graces; however, the "end of Holy Communion" is even greater still, "which is to make us partakers of Christ." For Wesley, the gift of forgiveness, sustenance, holiness, and eternal life are available to believers in the Eucharist because Jesus is really present: "I want and seek my saviour himself, and I haste to his sacrament . . . because I hope to find him there."[39] Wesley has a strong notion of divine presence, while distancing himself in some respects from Catholic teaching.

First, God uses ordinary means as instruments of his grace, and although the bread "hath nothing in itself, which can impart grace, holiness, and salvation" and Wesley does not know the "manner" that Christ is present, he does know that he is comforted and transformed in the meal.[40]

Second, it is by his senses (not despite them) that Wesley trusts the words of the Lord in receiving the sacrament. The instruments of the Old Testament were trustworthy means of God's grace and power, as is water for baptism. The bread and wine function similarly but with the highest end: "And when thou sayest, Go, take and eat this bread which I have blessed, I will doubt no more of being fed with the Bread of Life, than if I were eating thy very flesh."[41] Both the pope and Wesley trust that Jesus is present in the sacrament, and Wesley does so on the basis of the bread and wine that Jesus appointed for this purpose.

Third, Wesley is notoriously unclear in his metaphysics of presence.[42] On the one hand, by what "Hymn 63" rejects, he seems to think mistakenly that Catholics teach Christ's localized presence in the elements: "No local deity we worship, Lord, in thee."[43] On the other hand (and only very briefly in this text), he gestures toward a sense of real-yet-non-localized presence: "So that we need not say, Who will go up into heaven? since without either ascending or descending, this sacred body of Jesus fills with atonement and blessing the remotest parts of this temple."[44]

39. Wesley, CCS, 13.

40. Ibid., 14.

41. Ibid.,

42. Wesley's position is commonly referred to as a kind of virtualism or receptionism that is pneumatologically mediated. For a very helpful overview, see Khoo, *Wesleyan eucharistic Spirituality*, 55–73. However—and what calls for more discussion—is Cummings's analysis of Wesley's language of Jesus' body and blood as sacramentally present; see "John Wesley and eucharistic Ecclesiology," 147–48.

43. Wesley, HLS, 47.

44. Wesley, CSS, 15.

Fourth, what Wesley does clearly affirm is Christ's real presence in the sacrament and in the elements proper. He writes, "This Victim having been offered up in the fullness of times, and in the midst of the world, which is Christ's great temple, and having been thence carried up to heaven, which is his sanctuary; from thence spreads salvation all around . . . And thus his body and blood have everywhere, but especially at this sacrament, a true and real presence."[45] He makes an equally strong affirmation of Jesus' presence in the elements in "Hymn 30": "The cup of blessing blest by thee / let it thy blood impart; / the bread thy mystic body be, / and cheer each languid heart."[46]

While the work of Christ in the Eucharist is the dominant theological focus in Wesley's text, the work of the Holy Spirit is not entirely forgotten. In fact, in *Hymns on the Lord's Supper* the work of the Holy Spirit is quite prominent.[47] Both the presence of Christ in the elements and the holiness he works in our lives are the result of the Spirit's actions. Observe the following:

> Come, Holy Ghost, thine influence shed, and realize the sign;
> Thy life infuse into the bread, thy power into the wine.
> Effectual let the tokens prove, and made by heavenly art,
> Fit channels to convey thy love to every faithful heart.[48]

As Geoffrey Wainwright notes, "The Holy Spirit is the Person who, as it were, 'applies' Christ to the Christian and to the church; or we may say that it is 'in the Holy Spirit' that Christ comes to the church."[49] Moreover, the Spirit realizes not some generic presence of Christ in the Eucharist but the "dying merit" of his passion and the "living faith" of his salvation. As "Hymn 16" notes,

> Come, Thou everlasting Spirit, bring to every thankful mind
> All the Saviour's dying merit, all his sufferings for mankind;

---

45. Ibid. Methodists' use of the elements tends to be as unclear as Wesley's metaphysics. The elements may not change ontologically, but they are often treated with less dignity than standard table fare: for instance, the sanctuary floor may be littered with crumbs and the "leftovers" thrown out in the trash.

46. Wesley, *HLS*, 24.

47. See Stevick's discussion in *The Altar's Fire*, 121–25, where he notes the influence of Thomas Deacon and Jeremy Taylor on Wesley's pneumatology.

48. Wesley, *HLS*, 51.

49. Wainwright, *Eucharist and Eschatology*, 135.

True Recorder of his passion, now the living faith impart,
Now reveal his great salvation, preach his gospel to our heart.[50]

In the closing prayer of Section VII of *The Christian Sacrament and Sacrifice*, Wesley asks the Father to "bestow" a portion of "that Spirit, through which Thy Son offered Himself," in order to "sanctify" not just Christ's presence or the elements, but "the body of soul which [he] now offer[s]." The Spirit is asked to bring a "spirit of contrition," a "loathing" for sin, a "spirit of holiness," a release from temptation, and a union with Christ's cross in order that believers may "partake of one Passion, and enjoy with [God the Father] the same glory."[51] "Hymn 151" picks up the same prayer and words: "Come, Thou Spirit of contrition, / fill our souls with tender fears . . . Then we live to God forever, then in heaven on earth we live."[52]

When John Paul and John Wesley stress the presence of Christ in the Eucharist—albeit in different modalities—it is the presence of the risen and glorified Christ that they stress, whose death wins forgiveness and whose resurrection brings the imprint of the divine image onto the human nature, making Christians partakers of the divine nature. The holiness that God commands and that Christians desire comes to the repentant sinner through the Spirit in the form of Christ himself. In the intimacy of the communion meal, Jesus feeds his people with his divine life, thereby making them into what he has become.

Christ Will Come Again

The whole of Christ's person and work bear an indelibly eschatological dimension since everything Christ is and does is directed toward the ends that God has designed. As such, Jesus' sacrificial dying and rising not only represent and convey the pardon and power of new life to believers, but as the first fruits of the resurrection, his incorruptible body and perfect love of the Father are a foreshadowing of the final holiness for which Christians hope. As a foretaste of the heavenly banquet, the Eucharist serves as a pledge of our anticipated resurrection. Moreover, Jesus' presence in the Eucharist

---

50. Wesley, *HLS*, 13.

51. Wesley, *CSS*, 28–29. Holiness, though, is a process: in "Hymn 83," even after forgiveness and justification, there is yet a ways to go: "Still we are not new-created / still we are not sanctified / Thou to some in great compassion / Hast in part their sight restored / show us all thy full salvation / make the servants as their Lord" (*HLS*, 71).

52. Wesley, *HLS*, 127.

unites all the members of his body: the church in heaven with the church below. Finally, communion with the glorified Lord is transformative: Those who feast on him with repentance and faith learn to live a eucharistic life— a life of holiness—one that issues in sacrificial living in imitation of Jesus.

It is the Christ who has gone before them, who will come again, who comes to believers in the Eucharist, and who shares with his church his promise of resurrection. The pope's remarks on this acclamation are brief, and although they are as much anticipatory as they are precise, they nonetheless affirm the eschatological hope of the sacrament. "The Eucharist is a straining towards the goal," he writes, "a foretaste of the fullness of joy promised by Christ; it is in some way the anticipation of heaven, the pledge of future glory."[53] The Eucharist is marked by joyful, hopeful, and "confident waiting." Methodists could easily attribute such language to Wesley himself. Salvation is not only something believers anticipate in hope; the Eucharist communicates salvation now because the Eucharist communicates the Savior. "Those who feed on Christ in the Eucharist need not wait until the hereafter to receive eternal life; *they already possess it on earth*, as the first-fruits of a future fullness which will embrace man in his totality."[54] It is Catholic teaching that Christ's sacramental presence corresponds to the state of his actual body when the rite is celebrated. So, hypothetically, had the apostles celebrated the Supper on that first Holy Saturday when Jesus was in the tomb, they would have received the dead and powerless presence of Christ.[55] In the church's actual celebration of the Eucharist, the precise opposite is indeed the case: "This pledge of the future resurrection comes from the fact that the flesh of the Son of Man, given as food, is his body in its glorious state after the resurrection. With the Eucharist we digest, as it were, the 'secret' of the resurrection."[56]

Because the *mysterium paschale* is an eschatological event, so also is the *mysterium eucharisticum*. To be in communion with Christ is to be in communion with the "church in heaven," for both liturgies celebrate the "sacrifice of the Lamb." The Eucharist shows the church an inkling of "heaven appearing on earth . . . a glorious ray of the heavenly Jerusalem," guiding the church through the "clouds" of its earthly journey.[57]

53. John Paul II, *EE*, 18.
54. Ibid., 18; italics original.
55. See, for example, Thomas Aquinas, *ST*, 3.76.2 (5:2450) and 3.81.4 (5:2497).
56. John Paul II, *EE*, 18.
57. Ibid., 19.

Does the foretaste of the resurrection in the Eucharist and the anticipation of being united to the saints in glory render Christians complacent, meandering through this life while they look forward to the next? By no means! To have in the Eucharist the pledge of future glory and "the seed of living hope" strengthens Christians on their journey in this life. Without losing sight of the new heaven and the new earth, Christians must recognize the "work" needed now in this millennium; they have a "commitment," a "responsibility," and a "duty" to share in "the building of a more human world, a world fully in harmony with God's plan."[58] John Paul II draws from Jesus' foot-washing (John 13) and Paul's exhortation to unity (1 Cor 11) in order to sketch the church's commitment to topics such as peace, justice and solidarity, the integrity of human life, and the issue of poverty in a globalized world. In short, the presence of the risen Christ and the church's eschatological hope motivate and direct the church's witness and mission. "Proclaiming the death of the Lord 'until he comes' (1 Cor 11:26) entails that all who take part in the Eucharist be committed to changing their lives and making them in a certain way completely 'eucharistic.'"[59]

As a "pledge of future glory," the "third use" of the sacrament for Wesley turns out to be the "crown of the other two," even while all three uses "aim at the same glory." The final purpose of the Eucharist is to assure believers that what God did in Christ and has begun to do in his people God will faithfully bring to completion at the right time, namely the "eternal happiness" of seeing Christ face to face.[60] The life of "absolute redemption from death and our miseries" is "reserved" for Christians at the eschaton,[61] those who in this life are still too sinful, young, and weak "to bear the weight of eternal glory."[62] Christians commit their lives to him and trust that God will ultimately bring them into the heavenly kingdom. They do, however, enjoy Christ in reality and God's kingdom in foretaste here and now: "Christ and his estate, his happiness and his glory, his eternity and his heaven . . . the Body and Blood of Jesus, is in full value, and heaven with all

58. Ibid., 20.

59. Ibid.

60. See Wesley, CSS, 18. With respect to this eschatological dimension in the Eucharist as a pledge and foretaste of heaven, Wainwright demonstrates a common teaching between Wesley and the pope; "'Ecclesia de eucharistia vivit,'" 3–4. Wainwright credits HLS with recovering for the Western church a "rich appreciation" for the Eucharist in eschatological perspective (*Eucharist and Eschatology*, 70–72).

61. Wesley, CSS, 10.

62. Ibid., 18.

its glory" received by the communicants in the bread and wine.[63] Wesley is clear throughout Section V of *The Christian Sacrament and Sacrifice* that although Christians do not yet enjoy the fullness of the resurrection, their partaking of the risen Christ bestows "the virtue of it into [their] souls on earth."[64] Those who partake of Christ are in the process of really being made holy: "O Lord Jesus, who hast ordained these mysteries for a communion of thy body, a means of thy grace, and a pledge of thy glory, settle me hereby in the communion of thy sufferings which they show forth; feed me with that living bread which they present, and sanctify me in body and spirit for that eternal happiness which they promise."[65]

Although Wesley does not develop an ecclesiology here, his vision is thoroughly communal in scope, and he does have a doctrine of the *totus Christus*, that is, the church in heaven and on earth united to its head. The kingdom of God encompasses fellowship in both the church and in heaven, the former preparing the way for the latter "as the holy place to the holiest." Christ's disciples can have confidence in their eschatological feasting with Christ based on the trustworthiness of their eucharistic feasting on earth: "Whosoever, therefore, are admitted to this dinner of the Lamb, unless they be wanting to themselves, need not doubt of being admitted to the Marriage Supper of him who was dead, but now liveth for evermore."[66] "Hymn 112" moves from incomplete earthly holiness to eternal heavenly holiness:

> O that we now thy flesh may eat
> It's virtue really receive,
> Empower'd by this immortal meat
> The life of holiness to live:
> Partakers of thy sacrifice
> O may we all thy nature share,
> Till to the holiest place we rise
> And keep the feast forever there.[67]

---

63. Ibid., 19. See also "Hymn 103": "Title to eternal bliss / Here his precious death we find / This the pledge the earnest this / Of the purchased joys behind: / Here he gives our souls a taste / Heaven into our hearts he pours; / Still believe, and hold him fast / God and Christ and all is ours!" (*HLS*, 89).

64. Wesley, CSS, 18.

65. Ibid., 19.

66. Ibid., 17–18. Note that it is through the pastor that the authority and grace of the Eucharist are administered since "the minister of Christ [has] as much power from his Master for doing this, as any prophet ever had for what he did" (ibid., 19).

67. Wesley, *HLS*, 95.

A proper understanding of Christ's eschatological work in the Eucharist impinges directly on the worship of the church and on the lives of its members. Namely, who Christ was and has become affects intimately who his followers are becoming and what they will be like. Sacramentally, Christians are to conform to the one with whom they have saving communion. Wesley rebuts the idea that the only sacrifice "under the Gospel" is Christ's on the cross; unless Christians offer themselves in sacrifice, he asserts, they can neither receive nor share in Christ's redemption. The whole purpose of Christ's actions is to incorporate the members of his body into his work: "Jesus Christ does nothing without his Church, insomuch that sometimes they are represented as only one person."[68]

Wesley stresses the language of self-sacrifice and offering in order for the church to conform to Christ and to be united to him since what Christ did for his people he does not do now without them. In offering the Eucharist to God and themselves along with it, Christians are as a body incorporated into Christ's work, which is eternally a work of offering, intersession, and redemption. Just as the commemorative sacrifice of the Eucharist makes present the redeeming sacrifice of the cross, so the Christian's self-offering in time unites to Christ's eternity in the Godhead: In these acts, "Jesus Christ and all his members may jointly appear before God, that [they] may offer up [their] souls and bodies, at the same time, in the same place and in the same oblation."[69] This sacramental conformity to Christ transforms believers such that they become what apart from him they could never be: sanctified, hallowed, and consecrated. Indeed, conformity with Christ in worship and life is necessary if the eschatological pledge of future glory is ever to be realized.

Conformity with Christ is not limited to believers' self-offering in the sacrament; in addition to themselves, it is incumbent upon them to "bring the freewill-offering of their goods." This latter sacrifice readily follows the first, since the sacrifice of their possessions and actions flows directly from the sacrifice of their being. If believers can receive the immeasurable gift of Christ himself and all he "possesses" (that is, his grace, immortality, and glory), then in giving themselves to him they also, by extension, give him all their possession to be used for his glory.

Wesley never loses sight of the transforming power that results in communion with Christ: sacrificed goods are consecrated, multiplied, and

---

68. Wesley, CSS, 24.
69. Ibid., 27.

put to divine use. For the human person, the transformation is not only functional, but ontological and eschatological. To be united to Christ's "everlasting sacrifice of himself" in the Eucharist yields blessings beyond words, namely, being raised "to the very nature, the holiness, and immortality of God."[70] "Hymn 155" sums up all that the believer is, does, and offers to God for restoration and transformation:

> Take my soul and body's powers
> Take my mem'ry, mind, and will,
> All my goods, and all my hours
> All I know, and all I feel,
> All I think, and speak, and do
> Take my heart—but make it new.[71]

Conclusion

The church's eucharistic acclamation of the mystery of faith encapsulates Christ's paschal mystery, which is enacted in all its fullness and power in the eucharistic mystery. It is not hard to see why John Paul and John Wesley write as passionately and affectionately as they do about the Eucharist or why they place the sacrament at the center of Christian practice and urge their people to join in it frequently. Through the Holy Spirit Christians receive all the merits of Christ's sacrificial death, namely, forgiveness, justification, and reconciliation with God. Moreover, communion with Christ is transformative: by feasting on their glorified Lord, the members of his body participate in the triune life, and by offering themselves sacrificially with Christ to the Father, they participate in the Spirit's work of being renewed into the image of their head. Whatever differences John Paul and John Wesley may have (some substantial, some minor), they are subsumed under their common soteriology of Christ's work in the Eucharist as the cause of holiness in the Christian life. Together they call the church to work for holiness in heart and life by finding it in communion with the triune God.

---

70. Ibid., 30–31.
71. Wesley, *HLS*, 130.

Bibliography

Abraham, William J. "Christian Perfection." In *The Oxford Handbook of Methodist Studies*, edited by William J. Abraham and James E. Kirby, 587–601. Oxford: Oxford University Press, 2009.

———. "The End of Wesleyan Theology." *Wesleyan Theological Journal* 40 (2005) 7–25.

Allen, Richard. *The Life, Experience, and Gospel Labors of the Rt. Rev. Richard Allen*. Philadelphia: Ford and Riply, 1880.

Andrews, Dee E. *The Methodists and Revolutionary America, 1760–1800: The Shaping of an Evangelical Culture*. Princeton: Princeton University Press, 2000.

Aquinas, Thomas. *Lectura super Mattheum*. Corpus Thomisticum. 2011. http://www.corpusthomisticum.org/cma0500.html. Accessed February 7, 2017.

Arnett, William M. "The Role of the Holy Spirit in Entire Sanctification in the Writings of John Wesley." *Wesleyan Theological Journal* 14 (1979) 15–30.

"The Articles of Religion of the Methodist Episcopal Church." In *Creeds and Confessions of Faith in the Christian Tradition*, edited by Jaroslav Pelikan and Valerie Hotchkiss, 3:201–7. New Haven: Yale University Press, 2003.

Asbury, Francis. Journal Entry, "12 September 1771." In *The Journal and Letters of Francis Asbury*, edited by Elmer T. Clark, J. Manning Potts, and Jacob S. Payton, 1:4. Nashville: Abingdon, 1958.

Augustine. *Epistularum 190*. In *Epistulae. CSEL*, edited by A. Goldbacher, 44:155–234. Vienna: Tempsky, 1904.

———. *Homilies on the Gospel of John, 1–40*. Translated by Edmund Hill. Works of Saint Augustine: A New Translation for the 21st Century III/12. Hyde Park, NY: New City, 2009.

———. *Letters 100–155*. Translated by Roland Teske. Works of Saint Augustine: A New Translation for the 21st Century II/2. Hyde Park, NY: New City, 2003.

———. *Sermons on the New Testament 148–183*. Translated by Edmund Hill. Works of Saint Augustine: A New Translation for the 21st Century III/5. New Rochelle, NY: New City, 1992.

———. *Tractates on the Gospel of John 11–27*. Translated by John W. Rettig. Fathers of the Church 79. Washington, DC: Catholic University of America Press, 1998.

———. *Tractates on the Gospel of John 28–54*. Translated by John W. Rettig. Fathers of the Church 88. Washington, DC: Catholic University of America Press, 2010.

———. *Tractates on the Gospel of John 55–111*. Translated by John W. Rettig. Fathers of the Church 90. Washington, DC: Catholic University of America Press, 2010.

Bibliography

Baker, Anthony. *Diagonal Advance*. Eugene, OR: Cascade, 2011.

Balthasar, Hans Urs von. *Convergences: To the Source of Christian Mystery*. San Francisco, Ignatius, 1988.

Balthasar, Hans Urs von, and Karl Barth. *Einheit und Erneuerung der Kirche*. Freiburg: Paulusverlag, 1968.

Bangs, Carl. *Phineas F. Bresee: His Life in Methodism, the Holiness Movement, and the Church of the Nazarene*. Kansas City: Beacon Hill, 1995.

Barnes, Michel R. "Anti-Arian Works." In *Augustine through the Ages: An Encyclopedia*, edited by Allan D. Fitzgerald, 31–34. Grand Rapids: Eerdmans, 1999.

Bassett Paul M., ed. *Holiness Teaching: New Testament Times to Wesley*. Kansas City: Beacon Hill, 1997.

Bassett, Paul M., and William M. Greathouse. *Exploring Christian Holiness*. Vol. 2, *The Historical Development*. Kansas City: Beacon Hill, 1985.

Berrouard, Marie-François. *Introduction aux homélies de Saint Augustin sur l'Evangile de Saint Jean*. Paris: Études Augustiniennes, 2004.

Bonner, Gerald. "Augustine's Conception of Deification." *Journal of Theological Studies*, NS 37 (1986) 369–86.

The Book of Discipline of The United Methodist Church, 1972. Nashville: United Methodist Publishing House, 1973.

The Book of Discipline of The United Methodist Church, 1984. Nashville: United Methodist Publishing House, 1984.

The Book of Discipline of The United Methodist Church, 2012. Nashville: United Methodist Publishing House, 2012.

Borgen, Ole. *John Wesley on the Sacraments: A Theological Study*. Nashville: Abingdon, 1972.

Brown, Peter. *Augustine of Hippo: A Biography*. New ed. Berkeley: University of California Press, 2000.

———. *Religion and Society in the Age of Saint Augustine*. New York: Harper & Row, 1972.

Burnell, Peter. "Concupiscence and Moral Freedom in Augustine and before Augustine." *Augustinian Studies* 26 (1995) 49–63.

Burns, J. Patout. "Grace." In *Augustine through the Ages: An Encyclopedia*, edited by Allan D. Fitzgerald, 391–98. Grand Rapids: Eerdmans, 1999.

Calvin, John. *Institutes of the Christian Religion*. Edited by John T. McNeill. Translated by Ford Lewis Battles. Library of Christian Classics 20–21. Philadelphia: Westminster, 1960.

Campbell, Ted A. *John Wesley and Christian Antiquity: Religious Vision and Cultural Change*. Nashville: Kingswood, 1991.

———. "John Wesley on the Mission of the Church." In *The Mission of the Church in Methodist Perspective*, edited by Alan G. Padgett, 45–62. Studies in the History of Missions 10. Lewiston, NY: Mellen, 1992.

———. "The Transgressions of Gerasimos Avlonites." Published through the SMU Digital Repository, *Perkins Faculty Research and Special Events*, paper 3. http://digitalrepository.smu.edu/theology_research/3. Accessed February 8, 2017.

———. *Wesleyan Beliefs: Formal and Popular Expressions of the Core Beliefs of Wesleyan Communities*. Nashville: Kingswood, 2010.

Bibliography

———. "The 'Wesleyan Quadrilateral': The Story of a Modern Methodist Myth." *Doctrine and Theology in The United Methodist Church*, edited by Thomas A. Langford, 154–61. Nashville: Kingswood, 1991.

Cantalamessa, Raniero. *Beatitudes: Eight Steps to Happiness.* Cincinnati: Servant, 2009.

Cartwright, Peter. *Autobiography of Peter Cartwright.* New York: Abingdon, 1986.

Chapman, David. *In Search of the Catholic Spirit: Methodists and Roman Catholics in Dialogue.* Peterborough, UK: Epworth, 2004.

Charry, Ellen T. *God and the Art of Happiness.* Grand Rapids: Eerdmans, 2010.

Chiles, Robert E. *Theological Transition in American Methodism, 1790–1935.* Nashville: Abingdon, 1965.

Collins, Kenneth J. *The Theology of John Wesley: Holy Love and the Shape of Grace.* Nashville: Abingdon, 2007.

Colón-Emeric, Edgardo. *Wesley, Aquinas, and Christian Perfection: An Ecumenical Dialogue.* Waco: Baylor University Press, 2009.

Common Worship: Services and Prayers for the Church of England. London: Church House, 2000.

"Council of Ephesus." In *Decrees of the Ecumenical Councils*, edited by Norman P. Tanner, 1:37–74. Washington, DC: Georgetown University Press, 1990.

"Council of Nicaea." *Decrees of the Ecumenical Councils*, edited by Norman P. Tanner, 1:1–19. Washington, DC: Georgetown University Press, 1990.

Cummings, Brian, ed. *The Book of Common Prayer: The Texts of 1549, 1559, and 1662.* Oxford: Oxford University Press, 2011.

Cummings, Owen. "John Wesley and Eucharistic Ecclesiology." *One in Christ* 35 (1999) 143–51.

Deschner, John. *Wesley's Christology: An Interpretation.* Dallas: Southern Methodist University Press, 1985.

The Doctrine and Discipline of the African Methodist Episcopal Church, 2012. Nashville: AMEC Sunday School Union, 2013.

The Doctrines and Discipline of the African Methodist Episcopal Zion Church, 2008. Charlotte, NC: A.M.E. Zion Publishing House, 2008.

The Doctrines and Discipline of the Methodist Episcopal Church in America. With Explanatory Notes by Thomas Coke and Francis Asbury. Philadelphia: Tuckniss, 1798.

Dorrien, Gary. *The Making of American Liberal Theology: Imagining Progressive Religion, 1805–1900.* Louisville: Westminster John Knox, 2001.

Drinkhouse, Edward J. *History of Methodist Reform, Synoptical of General Methodism, 1703 to 1898.* 2 vols. Baltimore: Board of Publication of the Methodist Protestant Church, 1899.

English, John C. "References to St. Augustine in the Works of John Wesley." *Asbury Theological Journal* 60 (2005) 5–24.

Felton, Gayle Carlton. *This Holy Mystery: A United Methodist Understanding of Holy Communion.* Nashville: Discipleship Resources, 2005.

Finke, Roger, and Rodney Stark. *The Churching of America, 1776–2005: Winners and Losers in Our Religious Economy.* New Brunswick: Rutgers University Press, 2005.

Girvin, E. A. *Phineas Bresee: A Prince of Israel: A Biography.* Kansas City: Nazarene Publishing House, 1916.

Gunter, W. Stephen, et al., eds. *Wesley and the Quadrilateral: Renewing the Conversation.* Nashville: Abingdon, 1997.

Bibliography

Hatch, Nathan O. *The Democratization of American Christianity*. New Haven: Yale University Press, 1989.

———. "The Puzzle of American Methodism." In *Methodism and the Shaping of American Culture*, edited by Nathan O. Hatch and John H. Wigger, 25–27. Nashville: Kingswood, 2001.

Healy, Nicholas M. *Church, World and Christian Life: Practical-Prophetic Ecclesiology*. Cambridge: Cambridge University Press, 2000.

Heitzenrater, Richard P. "At Full Liberty: Doctrinal Standards in Early American Methodism." In *Mirror and Memory: Reflections on Early Methodism*, 189–204. Nashville: Kingswood, 1989.

———. "In Search of Continuity and Consensus: The Road to the 1988 Doctrinal Statement." In *Doctrine and Theology in the United Methodist Church*, edited by Thomas A. Langford, 93–108. Nashville: Kingswood, 1991.

Hulley, Leonard D. "An Interpretation of John Wesley's Doctrine of Perfect Love." *Theologia Evangelica* 13 (1990) 21–29.

Journet, Charles Cardinal. *The Mass: The Presence of the Sacrifice of the Cross*. South Bend: Saint Augustine's, 2008.

Khoo, Lorna Lock-Nah. *Wesleyan Eucharistic Spirituality: Its Nature, Sources and Future*. Adelaide: ATF, 2005.

Kilgore, Charles Franklin. "The James O'Kelly Schism in the Methodist Episcopal Church." PhD diss., Emory University, 1961.

Kirby, James E., Russell E. Richey, and Kenneth E. Rowe. *The Methodists*. Westport: Greenwood, 1996.

Knudson, Albert C. *The Doctrine of God*. Nashville: Abingdon, 1930.

Langford, Thomas A. "John Wesley's Doctrine of Sanctification." *Bulletin of the United Church of Canada Committee on Archives and History* 29 (1980–1982) 63–73.

———. *Practical Divinity: Theology in the Wesleyan Tradition*. Nashville: Abingdon, 1983.

Le Bruyns, Clint. "*Ecclesia de Eucharistia*: On its Ecumenical Import." *Ecumenical Trends* 32 (2003) 120–125.

Lee, Jesse. *A Short History of the Methodists in the United States of America: Beginning in 1776, and Continued till 1809*. Baltimore: Magill and Clime, 1810.

Lindström, Harald. *Wesley and Sanctification: A Study in the Doctrine of Salvation*. Stockholm: Nya Bokförlags Aktiebolaget, 1946.

Lloyd, Gareth. *Charles Wesley and the Struggle for Methodist Identity*. Oxford: Oxford University Press, 2007.

Long, D. Stephen. *John Wesley's Moral Theology: The Quest for God and Goodness*. Nashville: Kingswood, 2005.

Looney, Thomas. "Ecumenical 'Lights' and 'Shadows' in *Ecclesia de Eucharistia*." *Ecumenical Trends* 32 (2003) 97–108.

Loyer, Kenneth M. "'And to Crown All': John Wesley on Union with God in the New Creation." *Methodist Review* 1 (2009) 109–25.

———. *God's Love through the Spirit: The Holy Spirit in Thomas Aquinas and John Wesley*. Washington, DC: Catholic University of America Press, 2014.

MacIntyre, Alasdair. *Whose Justice? Which Rationality?* Notre Dame: University of Notre Dame Press, 1988.

Maddox, Randy L. "The Enriching Role of Experience." In *Wesley and the Quadrilateral: Renewing the Conversation*, edited by W. Stephen Gunter et al., 107–27. Nashville: Abingdon, 1997.

Bibliography

———. *Responsible Grace: John Wesley's Practical Theology*. Nashville: Kingswood, 1994.

Martin, Robert K. "Toward a Wesleyan Sacramental Ecclesiology." *Ecclesiology* 9 (2013) 19–38.

McConnell, Francis J. *Borden Parker Bowne: His Life and His Philosophy*. New York: Abingdon, 1929.

Meconi, David Vincent. *The One Christ: St. Augustine's Theology of Deification*. Washington, DC: Catholic University of America Press, 2013.

Meistad, Tore. *Martin Luther and John Wesley on the Sermon on the Mount*. Lanham, MD: Scarecrow, 1999.

Mil Voces para Celebrar. Nashville: United Methodist Publishing House, 1996.

Miles, Rebekah L. "Happiness, Holiness, and the Moral Life." In *The Cambridge Companion to John Wesley*, edited by Randy L. Maddox and Jason E. Vickers, 207–24. Cambridge: Cambridge University Press, 2010.

Moore, D. Marselle. "Development in Wesley's Thought on Sanctification and Perfection." *Wesleyan Theological Journal* 20 (1985) 29–53.

Nisula, Timo. *Augustine and the Functions of Concupiscence*. Supplements to Vigiliae Christianae 116. Leiden: Brill, 2012.

O'Malley, J. Steven, and Jason E. Vickers, eds. *Methodist and Pietist: Retrieving the Evangelical United Brethren Tradition*. Nashville: Kingswood, 2011.

"Our Theological Task." In *The Book of Discipline of The United Methodist Church, 1972*, 68–82. Nashville: United Methodist Publishing House, 1973.

Outler, Albert C. "Introduction" to "Christian Perfection." WJW 2:98.

———. "Introduction to the Report of the 1968–72 Theological Study Commission." In *Doctrine and Theology in The United Methodist Church*, edited by Thomas A. Langford, 20–25. Nashville: Kingswood, 1991.

———. "John Wesley's Interests in the Early Fathers of the Church." *Bulletin of the United Church of Canada Committee on Archives and History Bulletin* 29 (1980–1982) 5–17.

———. "A New Future for Wesley Studies: An Agenda for 'Phase III.'" In *The Wesleyan Theological Heritage: Essays of Albert C. Outler*, edited by Thomas C. Oden and Leicester R. Longden, 132–37. Grand Rapids: Zondervan, 1991.

———. "Upon Our Lord's Sermon on the Mount." WJW, 1:466–69.

———. "The Wesleyan Quadrilateral—In John Wesley." In *Doctrine and Theology in The United Methodist Church*, edited by Thomas A. Langford, 75–88. Nashville: Kingswood, 1991.

Outler, Albert C., ed. *John Wesley*. New York: Oxford University Press, 1980.

Palmer, Phoebe. *The Way of Holiness*. London: Heylin, 1856.

Peters, John L. *Christian Perfection and American Methodism*. Grand Rapids: Asbury, 1985.

Pieper, Josef. *In Tune with the World: A Theory of Festivity*. New York: Harcourt, Brace & World, 1965.

Pilario, Daniel Franklin E. "Eucharist and Human Suffering: Retrieving 'Sacrifice' in the Contemporary Magisterium." *Modern Theology* 30 (2014) 340–56.

Pinckaers, Servais. *The Sources of Christian Ethics*. Washington, DC: Catholic University of America Press, 1995.

Possidius, *The Life of Saint Augustine*. Translated by Herbert T. Weiskotten. Merchantville, NJ: Evolution, 2008.

Richardson, John. "Letter to Charles Wesley, 13 March 1764." Manuscript copy in the John Rylands University Library of Manchester. "MAM MA 1977/502."

Bibliography

Richey, Russell E. *Early American Methodism*. Bloomington: Indiana University Press, 1991.

Richey, Russell E., Kenneth E. Rowe, and Jean Miller Schmidt. *The Methodist Experience in America*. 2 vols. Nashville: Abingdon, 2000–2010.

Rist, John M. *Augustine: Ancient Thought Baptized*. New York: Cambridge University Press, 1994.

Roberts, B. T. "New School Methodism." In *Populist Saints: B. T. and Ellen Roberts and the First Free Methodists*, by Howard A. Snyder, 389–95. Grand Rapids: Eerdmans, 2006.

———. *Why Another Sect*. Rochester: "The Earnest Christian," 1879.

Runyon, Theodore. *The New Creation: John Wesley's Theology Today*. Nashville: Abingdon, 1998.

Ruth, Lester. *A Little Heaven Below: Worship at Early Methodist Quarterly Meetings*. Nashville: Kingswood, 2000.

Schlimm, Matthew R. "The Puzzle of Perfection: Growth in John Wesley's Doctrine of Perfection." *Wesleyan Theological Journal* 38 (2003) 124–42.

Scott, Orange. "The Grounds of Secession from the M. E. Church." Excerpt found in *The Methodist Experience in America*, by Russell E. Richey, Kenneth E. Rowe, and Jean Miller Schmidt, 2:257–59. Nashville: Abingdon, 2000.

Shults, F. LeRon, and Andrea Hollingsworth. *The Holy Spirit*. Grand Rapids: Eerdmans, 2008.

Simpson, Matthew. "The Centenary of American Methodism." In *The Life of Bishop Matthew Simpson of the Methodist Episcopal Church*, by George R. Crook, 505–12. New York: Harper & Bros., 1890.

Sprague, C. Joseph. *Affirmations of a Dissenter*. Nashville: Abingdon, 2002.

Snyder, Howard A. *Populist Saints: B. T. and Ellen Roberts and the First Free Methodists*. Grand Rapids: Eerdmans, 2006.

Sours, Stephen. "Eucharist and Anthropology: Seeking Convergence on Eucharistic Sacrifice between Catholics and Methodists." PhD diss., Duke University, 2011.

Staples, Rob L. *Outward Sign and Inward Grace: The Place of Sacraments in Wesleyan Spirituality*. Kansas City: Beacon Hill, 1991.

Steck, SJ, Christopher. "In Union with the Paschal Mystery: The Eucharist and Suffering in the Thought of John Paul II." In *Pope John Paul II on the Body: Human, Eucharistic, Ecclesial*, edited by John M. McDermott and John Gavin, 311–21. Philadelphia: Saint Joseph's University Press, 2007.

Steinmetz, David C. *Calvin in Context*. 2nd ed. New York: Oxford University Press, 2010.

Stevick, Daniel B. *The Altar's Fire: Charles Wesley's Hymns on the Lord's Supper, 1745 Introduction and Exposition*. Peterborough, UK: Epworth, 2004.

Strong, Douglas M. "American Methodism in the Nineteenth Century: Expansion and Fragmentation." In *The Cambridge Companion to American Methodism*, edited by Jason E. Vickers, 63–96. Cambridge: Cambridge University Press, 2013.

———. "Borden Parker Bowne and Henry Clay Morrison: Conflicting Conceptions of Twentieth Century Methodism." In *From Aldersgate to Azusa Street: Wesleyan, Holiness, and Pentecostal Visions of the New Creation*, edited by Henry H. Knight III, 297–306. Eugene, OR: Pickwick, 2010.

Stuhlman, Byron David. *Occasions of Grace: An Historical and Theological Study of the Pastoral Offices and Episcopal Services in the Book of Common Prayer*. New York: Church Hymnal, 1995.

The Sunday Service of the Methodists with Other Occasional Services. London: n.p., 1788.

Bibliography

Teasdale, Mark R. *Methodist Evangelism, American Salvation: The Home Missions of the Methodist Episcopal Church, 1860–1920.* Eugene, OR: Pickwick, 2014.

"The Thirty-Nine Articles of the Church of England." In *Creeds and Confessions of Faith in the Christian Tradition*, edited by Jaroslav Pelikan and Valerie Hotchkiss, 2:526–40. New Haven: Yale University Press, 2003.

Thompson, Andrew C. "Outler's Quadrilateral, Moral Psychology, and Theological Reflection in the Wesleyan Tradition." *Wesleyan Theological Journal* 46 (2011) 49–72.

Thorsen, Donald. *Calvin vs. Wesley: Bringing Belief in Line with Practice.* Nashville: Abingdon, 2013.

Torrell, Jean-Pierre. *Saint Thomas Aquinas.* Vol. 1, *The Person and His Work.* Washington, DC: Catholic University of America Press, 1996.

Vickers, Jason E. "American Methodism: A Theological Tradition." In *The Cambridge Companion to American Methodism*, 9–43. Cambridge: Cambridge University Press, 2013.

———. *Wesley: A Guide for the Perplexed.* London: T. & T. Clark, 2009.

Vincent, John Heyl. "The Autobiography of Bishop Vincent." *Northwestern Christian Advocate* 58 (6 April–2 November, 1910) n.p.

Vincent of Lérins. *Commonitorium.* Edited by Reginald Stewart Moxon. Cambridge Patristic Texts. Cambridge: Cambridge University Press, 1915.

Wadell, Paul J. *Happiness and the Christian Moral Life.* 2nd ed. Lanham, MD: Rowman and Littlefield, 2012.

Wainwright, Geoffrey. "'Ecclesia de eucharistia vivit': An Ecumenical Reading." *Ecumenical Trends* 33 (2004) 1–9.

———. *Eucharist and Eschatology.* Akron: OSL, 2002.

———. "Introduction." In *Hymns on the Lord's Supper*, by John and Charles Wesley, v–xiv. Facsimile ed. Madison, NJ: Charles Wesley Society, 1995.

———. *Methodists in Dialog.* Nashville: Kingswood, 1995.

Walsh, OP, Liam. "The Presence of the Mystery of Christ in the Broken Bread." In *The Mystery of Faith: Reflections on the Encyclical* Ecclesia de Eucharistia, edited by James McEvoy and Maurice Hogan, 140–60. Dublin: Columba, 2005.

Watson, David Lowes. *The Early Methodist Class Meeting: Its Origins and Significance.* Eugene, OR: Wipf and Stock, 1985.

Watson, Kevin M. *Pursuing Social Holiness: The Band Meeting in Wesley's Thought and Popular Methodist Experience.* New York: Oxford University Press, 2014.

Wesley, Charles. "I Want a Principle Within." *United Methodist Hymnal*, # 410. Nashville: United Methodist Publishing House, 1989.

Wesley, John. "An Address to the Clergy." *Works* 10:480–500.

———. "Brief Thoughts on Christian Perfection." *WJW* 13:199.

———. "Catholic Spirit." *WJW* 2:79–95.

———. "The Character of a Methodist." *WJW* 9:31–46.

———. "Christian Perfection." *WJW* 2:96–124.

———. "A Collection of Hymns for the Use of the People Called Methodists." *WJW* 7:71–722.

———. "Directions given to the Band Societies." *WJW* 9:79.

———. "The Duty of Constant Communion." *WJW* 3:427–39.

———. "The End of Christ's Coming." *WJW* 2:471–84.

———. *Explanatory Notes upon the New Testament.* London: Epworth, 1954.

———. "God's Love to Fallen Man." *WJW* 2:422–35.

Bibliography

———. "The Great Privilege of Those That are Born of God." WJW 1:431–43.

———. *John Wesley's Sunday Service of the Methodists in North America*. Reprint: Nashville: The United Methodist Publishing House and the United Methodist Board of Higher Education and Ministry, 1984.

———. Journal Entry, "11 June 1739." WJW 19:65–68.

———. Journal Entry, "13 September 1739." WJW 19:96–97.

———. Journal Entry, "22 June 1740." WJW 19:153–55.

———. Journal Entry, "27 June 1740." WJW 19:158.

———. "Justification by Faith." WJW 1:181–99.

———. "Letter to George Downing, 6 April 1761." WJW 27:249–50.

———. "Letter to John Mason, 21 November 1776." Telford 6:239–40.

———. "Letter to Mr. ----, 31 October 1789." Telford 8:182–83.

———. "Letter to Mrs. Maitland, 12 May 1763." Telford 4:212–13.

———. "Letter to Robert Carr Brackenbury, 15 September 1790." Telford 8:237–38.

———. "Letter to a Roman Catholic, 18 July 1749." Telford 3:7–14.

———. "The Life of Mr. Gregory Lopez." *A Christian Library consisting of Extracts from and Abridgments of the Choicest Pieces of Practical Divinity*, 27:387–438. London: Kershaw, 1826.

———. "The Means of Grace." WJW 1:376–97.

———. "Minutes of Several Conversations." Works 8:299–338.

———. "The Nature, Design, and General Rules of the United Societies." WJW 9:69–75.

———. "The New Birth." WJW 2:186–201.

———. "The New Creation." WJW 2:500–510.

———. "On Faith." WJW 3:491–501.

———. "On Laying the Foundation of the New Chapel, Near the City-Road, London." WJW 3:577–92.

———. "On Patience." WJW 3:169–79.

———. "On Perfection." WJW 3:70–87.

———. "On Sin in Believers." WJW 1:317–34.

———. "On Temptation." WJW 3:156–68.

———. "On the Trinity." WJW 2:373–86.

———. "On the Wedding Garment." WJW 4:139–48.

———. "On Working Out Our Own Salvation." WJW 3:199–209.

———. *A Plain Account of Christian Perfection*. Kansas City: Beacon Hill, 1966.

———. "A Plain Account of the People Called Methodists." WJW 9:254–80.

———. "Preface" to *Sermons on Several Occasions* (1746). WJW 1:103–7.

———. "The Principles of a Methodist Farther Explained." WJW 9:160–237.

———. "The Repentance of Believers." WJW 1:335–52.

———. "The Righteousness of Faith." WJW 1:200–216.

———. "Rules of the Band Societies." WJW 9:77–78.

———. "Salvation by Faith." WJW 1:117–30.

———. "The Scripture Way of Salvation." WJW 2:153–69.

———. "Spiritual Worship." WJW 3:89–102.

———. "Thoughts upon Methodism." WJW 9:527–30.

———. "To 'Our Brethren in America.'" In *John Wesley*, edited by Albert C. Outler, 82–84. New York: Oxford University Press, 1964.

———. "The Unity of the Divine Being." WJW 4:60–71.

———. "Upon Our Lord's Sermon on the Mount, I." WJW 1:469–87.

Bibliography

———. "Upon Our Lord's Sermon on the Mount, II." WJW 1:488–509.
———. "Upon Our Lord's Sermon on the Mount, III." WJW 1:510–30.
———. "Wesley's Interview with Bishop Butler." WJW 19:471–74.
———. "The Wisdom of God's Counsels." WJW 2:551–66.
Wigger, John. *American Saint: Francis Asbury and the Methodists*. New York: Oxford University Press, 2009.
———. *Taking Heaven by Storm: Methodism and the Rise of Popular Christianity in America*. Urbana: University of Illinois Press, 1998.
Williams, Colin W. *John Wesley's Theology Today*. Nashville: Abingdon, 1960.

www.ingramcontent.com/pod-product-compliance
Lightning Source LLC
Chambersburg PA
CBHW050818160426
43192CB00010B/1810